You Can't Coach Height

Growing Up Tall, Jewish, and Free
in the Mountains of North Carolina

Joe Kaplan

Mountain Page Press
Hendersonville, NC

Copyright © 2015 Joe Kaplan

2nd edition 2020

You Can't Coach Height
Growing Up Tall, Jewish, and Free in the Mountains of North Carolina
ISBN 978-1-952714-19-1

All rights reserved. No part of this publication may be reproduced, stored in a retrieval system, distributed, or transmitted in any form or by any means (electronic, mechanical, photocopying, recording, or otherwise) without prior written permission from the publisher. Book club or other group discounts available through publisher.

Mountain Page Press
118 5th Ave. W.
Hendersonville, NC 28792 Visit:

www.MountainPagePress.com

Cover design by Meghan McDonald
Watercolor painting on cover by Seymour R Kaplan

Printed in the United States

Dedication

---◆---

Because they should always know who they are and where they came from, this book is dedicated to Sue who has put up with my mishegaas* for 50 years, and to our sons, our grandchildren, our nieces and nephews, and those yet to come

*Mishegaas: One of those Yiddish words that has come into English usage that means any variation of: Foolishness, madness, folly, indulgence, frivolity, prank, madness, mess, etc. You get the idea.

Table of contents

Why I wrote this book 7
Prologue 9
How did we get to Canton anyway? 13
Canton 25
Growing up in Canton 35
Family history 67
Being Jewish in Canton 77
My bar mitzvah 91
The new store and more Canton stories 101
Cars and Trips 121
Asheville 131
Afterword 167

Why I wrote this book

I decided to write this book to pass on to my children and grandchildren, and those who follow them, some knowledge of who their parents and grandparents were, where they came from, and what the world was like for the generations that preceded them. I believe that history is very important and that knowing your own history is important in understanding the world around you.

I also wrote this book because, over the years, as I've gotten older and told people about my family and my life they say, "Joe, you know, you ought to write that down; really, you should start writing these stories and save them or they'll be forgotten; you have so much family history stored away." I have often thought that I should start writing these stories because I do seem to have a lot of memories about our family. Once I decided to start writing, the problem became knowing where to begin, there's just so much to think about; so much to think about.

Then, as I began the work, I realized that it was more than just a genealogy of who, what, and where, and I wanted to tell more of my own story—who I am and what it meant to grow up in a small southern town in the mountains. What it meant to be the only Jewish family in that town and what small-town life was like in a long-ago era where children had much more freedom to be themselves. Growing up then was so much different from today, especially in large urban areas. I feel there is an interesting story to tell. So, I decided that I would just start with myself.

Another part of the story is the Jewish history of the small towns of Western North Carolina. I include that as it also affected my growing up, how I see myself, and the person I have become as I related to most of the

Jewish families in the other small towns of Hendersonville, Sylva, Brevard, Murphy, Waynesville, and the big city, Asheville.

The original theme was to write a short history of where I came from and where my family came from to leave for my cildren and my grandchildren. But it started to grow and expand as my interest in history began to take over. I realized that I had to look into the historical background of who these people were, not just my immediate family, but those who influenced them, and from the people who influenced them on out to the world events that played on them to cause them to take the actions that they did.

From looking at who I am and where I came from, I realized that I also had to explore some of the historical and economic forces that drove the great migrations of not only the Jewish people of Eastern Europe but other oppressed people to these American shores. Paralleling that migration, were there similar economic forces playing on my family, specifically after the Second World War, causing them to move to the South and into western North Carolina from areas like northeastern Pennsylvania to find a new life for themselves?

From my simple desire to leave a story of my family to my children has come this complicated theme of historical and economic forces that drive societal change.

Prologue

Probably the only six-foot-tall bar mitzvah boy in all of North Carolina in October 1955, in the small mountain town of Canton, I was still growing steadily. My growth spurt started less than a year before, adding an inch or so a month, and wouldn't slow down until I was out of high school. I didn't top out at 6′5″ until I was out of the army at age 24. The beginning of 8th grade, in October 1955, was the month of my bar mitzvah—the celebration of a Jewish boy's 13th birthday that defines him as a man for Jewish ritual practice—finally, after months of study and preparation.

The 8th grade, and especially October 1955, was memorable for many reasons; the first of which is that I was part of the charter class in the new building, the annex that was built onto the old Canton High School building. This building housed the 7th and 8th grades, a new gym, and cafeteria. I was a proud member of the first 8th grade class. Secondly, On October 4, 1955, the Brooklyn Dodgers won the World Series at last, beating the New York Yankees 2-0. They'd lost the championship seven times already, and they'd lost five times just to the Yanks, in 1941, 1947, 1949, 1952, and 1953. But in 1955, thanks to nine brilliant innings in the seventh game from 23-year-old lefty pitcher Johnny Podres, they finally managed to beat the Bombers for the first, and last, time. The game was broadcast live over the school speaker system and our teacher let us listen to the whole game. Also that year, Tennessee Ernie Ford had a hit song called, *Sixteen Tons*, which was very popular among my friends and I remember memorizing all the lyrics. For some reason the song resonated with me and

I can never forget the line, "You owe your soul to the company store," sung in that deep baritone voice, one word, one syllable at a time.

Canton was a Company Store town built to support the Champion Paper and Fibre Company, where, not too many years earlier, employees were still being paid in scrip, the company's artificial currency, only redeemable at the Company Store. I remember my friends talking about buying things at the Company Store and Dad taking the scrip in lieu of payment at our auto parts store, even though he wasn't supposed to, and then somehow working a deal to redeem it at Champion.

I was also the tallest kid in the school. One day, early in the school year, I was walking down the hall and the coach of the basketball team stopped me. You have to understand that in those days, "Coach" was a venerated figure who seldom spoke to mere mortals like skinny 8th grad- ers. But, there I was, this tall, skinny kid and Coach was looking up at me saying something like, "Where did YOU come from?"

In this small town he had to have known every kid coming out of the two or three grammar schools, Pennsylvania Avenue School—Penn Ave.—where I was, North Canton, up by the mill where the tough, mean kids went, and Beaverdam. Coach must have had his eye on future football and basketball players and suddenly, here is this tall, skinny kid who is head and shoulders above everyone in the hallway and who has the one skill he can't coach into a player, height. I was skinny and clumsy and didn't have an athletic bone in my body, but coaches forever live with hopes and dreams.

I had no answer to his question and no clue what he was talking about, more afraid of him than anything else. He then asked if I played basketball, and my answer was something along the lines of, "What's that?" Up till that day, I don't think I had ever touched a basketball, let alone knew how to play, dribble, shoot, throw, or catch one. The sports we played were baseball and softball in the summer and tag football on any empty lot we could find in the fall until it got too cold.

Coach's next words were to tell me when and where to show up for practice; that I was "going out" for basketball. As things turned out, I did go out for basketball and played on the junior varsity (JV) team through the 10th grade. Coach must have been frustrated because I was pretty much uncoachable—I had no innate athletic skills. I couldn't jump, run fast, catch the ball reliably, or develop a decent jump shot. I succeeded in continuing to grow and was always the tallest kid in our conference. I loved being part of the team and wearing the uniforms on game days. We would line up for our grand entrance for warm-up drills before the games and the sound system would start playing *Sweet Georgia Brown* as we ran onto the court and into our warm-up routine. That was a great thrill; we always looked good in warm-ups. In the 10th grade we only lost two games and won the state JV championship. I did get a few minutes of play in most games and by the end of the 10th grade season I was allowed to dress with the varsity team a couple of times.

We never know how one part of our life will later have an effect on another. Fewer than 10 years later I found myself in Army Basic Training in Fort Gordon, Georgia. I believe that the physical training I had in those three years of playing basketball helped me get through the rigorous physical requirements of Basic. Coach believed in being in shape; in running, and running, and running. He wanted us to be running up and down the court at the end of the game as hard as the other team ran at the beginning. He worked us intensely and I credit him with helping me tremendously in building physical endurance. Not only that, but I was beginning to understand that it takes persistence to attempt to reach a goal, that you won't always be successful, that you have to reach for the goal anyway, and that teamwork is important in most endeavors. You have to learn to get along with everyone whether you like them or not, and you won't like everyone and they won't like you.

How did we get to Canton anyway?

The war ended

It was the end of the Second World War and the whole world was in a state of turmoil and disruption. Continents, nations, and families were torn up and destroyed. We were among the lucky ones as my father came home from the war in the Pacific in one piece both physically and mentally. Although we descended from Eastern European Jews, we know of no immediate family members who were murdered in the holocaust.

I don't know how Mom and Dad—Molly and Louis—actually met; I don't think we were ever told the story of who introduced them or the circumstances of their first date or anything like that. Mom was born and grew up in Scranton and Dad's family moved there from Greenport, New York, at some time when he was still a young boy (another story I don't know). They both came from very religious families so they may have travelled in the same social circles although I don't think either family had enough money to do very much socializing.

However they met and however long their courtship was, Dad was 30 when they married in March of 1939 and Mom was three years younger. Dad always liked to tell the story of how they took off on their honeymoon driving to Miami with exactly $100.00 in his pocket! They drove all the way to Miami Beach and back from Scranton, Pennsylvania.

Dad came home to Scranton to his wife Molly, two sons, Morty and Joe, and a new daughter, Judy, to a world at home that must have been incredibly frightening and uncertain. Although he had a law degree, he never sat for the bar exam and never had any interest in practicing law. Prior to the war, the extended family had lived on a farm in Montrose, PA, that my grandfather bought in the 1930s as a defense against the Great Depression. They had a small timber mill and hauled coal; they were hard workers who always took care of themselves. Grampa never believed in working for someone else and never let his sons do so. In fact, I believe that I was the first one in the extended family to ever work for someone else except for a short period when Dad worked in Connecticut. Mom married into this rather loud, argumentative, boisterous family and didn't get along—so I was told—with either her father-in-law and at least one of her brothers-in-law. "Didn't get along," is an understatement; I think she was afraid of them and they didn't treat her very well. So, when Dad came home and they looked around for where and how they were going to make a living, leaving Scranton, where they had all migrated back to during the war, was high on my parents' list.

There were four brothers on my father's side. Dad was the oldest, followed by Morris, Bernie, and Seymour. They all served in the Army except Bernie, who was exempt as the last son at home and working on a farm. As I understand the history of the war, there was a large hue and cry after a family lost all five sons who were allowed to serve together on a ship that was sunk.

After that, a policy was instituted whereby the last son was not taken.

It all started with Uncle Morris

The answer to the question, "How did we get to Canton?" begins with Uncle Morris and his time in the Army. It is a famous love story that is now part of the history of Hendersonville, North Carolina. But before I can tell that story, I have to tell you about Louis Williams.

Louis Williams' name was originally Louis Williamowsky. Without knowing about Louis Williams and his history, we cannot follow the chain of events that led to Dad and Mom coming to Canton. But, in order to examine those events, we have to look at the history of the Jewish Diaspora that goes back even further into Eastern Europe, which is a favorite topic of mine.

In the second of a three-volume history of the Jews of Eastern Europe entitled, *The Jews in Poland and Russia, Volume II: 1881 to 1914*,[1] by Antony Polonsky, the author provides a detailed and very readable history of the forces that drove my forebears and millions of others to these shores.

The thing that brings immigrants to this country from so many war-torn, poverty-stricken places is the promise of change—that their children, born in American optimism and American confidence, will no longer have the old hate, the old fear, the old memories. Without this kind of break from the past, multi-culturalism would not be possible at all. Descendants of the English and the Irish, or the Koreans and the Japanese, or other traditional enemies, could not live together in peace and friendship as Americans if they still cherished the old antagonisms.

The Jewish case is not quite the same as that of other groups. Jewishness is not only an ethnicity, it is also a religion, which means that practicing Jews automatically maintain a connection to the whole of Jewish history, as it is recorded in Scripture, the liturgy, and the calendar. The historical memory of the Jews comes to them through many avenues. More importantly, perhaps, in dictating American-Jewish attitudes toward Jewish history is the way the Holocaust profoundly altered the course of that history.

The period between 1881 and 1914 is especially interesting to American Jews because it was in exactly these years that most of our ancestors came to this country. "Starting in 1880," Polonsky writes, "some 2.2 million Jews left the Russian Empire, which included most of the

Polish Jewish heartland, and 1.75 million of them ended up in the United States. The exodus of Jews was so massive that, by 1920, by far the largest Ashkenazi (that is, those of European as opposed to Spanish and North African Descent, known as Sephardic) Jewish city in the world was New York, with 1.8 million Jews, compared to just 350,000 in Warsaw, the next largest."

Naturally, millions of people do not flee a country where they are happy, and the scale of Jewish emigration offers a sense of how desperate the Jews of Russia and Poland were becoming. That crisis began abruptly in 1881 when the relatively liberal Tsar Alexander II was assassinated by a revolutionary group. His successor, Alexander III, was a reactionary with a particular animus against Jews, and the beginning of his reign was marked by a wave of deadly pogroms.

Derived from the Russian word meaning, *to wreak havoc*, a pogrom is an organized attack, often a massacre, against a minority group, particularly Jews. In the Russian Empire the Jews had been subject to such persecutions for centuries, often at the instigation of local government officials. However, in the period between 1881 and the Russian Revolution they were especially violent. A typical pogrom lasted from one to several days. With astonishing brutality, peasants and even city folk would riot against their Jewish neighbors with little fear of punishment, looting and burning their synagogues and businesses. When the police finally intervened, little or no effort was made to apprehend the attackers and bring them to justice.

At the same time, the new Tsar approved the infamous May Laws, which prohibited Jews from living in villages or buying land. This "legislative pogrom," in the words of the great Russian Jewish historian Simon Dubnow, had the effect of concentrating the Jewish population in desperately poor towns and cities, causing an economic crisis. It also marked an end to the previous Russian policy of trying to assimilate the Jews into the

Russian empire. From that point on, the Jews were treated more or less openly as enemies by the Tsarist government. Polonsky writes that, "When advised to end the repression of the Jews, [the Tsar] had observed, 'But we must never forget that the Jews crucified our Lord and shed his precious blood.'"

Things were somewhat better in Austrian Poland, where millions of Jews lived in the province of Galicia, and even better in the small Prussian-ruled section of Poland, where—ironically, as it appears in retrospect—the Jews achieved the greatest degree of equality. But in each territory, Polonsky shows, the Jews energetically debated the best ways to adapt to the pressures of the modern world. Ultimately, the decision was to leave, primarily to America.[2]

Louis Williams (1889–1971) was born in Grodna, Poland. He emigrated to America through Galveston, Texas, in 1907 instead of the more usual route of Ellis Island, NY. It is not commonly known that a substantial minority of immigrants were diverted through Galveston when Ellis Island got too busy.

Most Americans are aware of the historical significance of Ellis Island as a symbol of America's great immigrant gateway. Not many, however are aware of the other entry points through which immigrants also flowed into this country. From the years 1907–1914 Galveston served as one of these important points of entry. The state of Texas supported what was formally known as the "Galveston Immigration Plan" that escorted thousands of Jewish immigrants through the gates into all parts of America to resettle. The Galveston Port was small and the program encouraged dispersion across Texas to as far north as Fargo, North Dakota. As we still see today, issues of immigration are as old as the country, and the debate still remains active as America remains true to its roots as an international country.

As the many thousands of Jews were choosing to emigrate and America was serving a major destination, most were settling in the large East Coast cities. Urban areas such as New York, Boston, and Philadelphia, however, suffered from severe overcrowding, and Jewish leaders worried that crime and poverty would lead to restrictions on immigration.

Jacob Schiff, a New York banker of German-Jewish origin and major philanthropist, worked to find a solution to the problem of congestion and to improve the living conditions of the Jews who were coming from Eastern Europe. His goal was to relieve the pressure of the congestion by encouraging the migrants to move to the empty interior of the country. He chose Galveston as a likely gateway city and created an organization called the Jewish Immigrant Information Bureau, and in New York he created the Galveston Committee. The committee worked with the Jewish aid organizations in Europe, England, and Russia to recruit immigrants to go to Galveston instead of to New York. Galveston was chosen for its small size as a way of encouraging the new arrivals to disperse, thus avoiding the possibility of overcrowding. Also, it was a regular port of call for the shipping line that served Bremen, Germany, which was the main embarkation point for European Jewish migrants.

In 1907, 900 immigrants passed through Galveston even though the entry point building burned down two days before the first boat was scheduled to arrive. However, the mayor of Galveston was a big supporter of the program and he spoke to the first group of 56 immigrants. From Galveston the immigrants were sent to various western states and many stayed in towns throughout Texas including Fort Worth, Cleburne, Texarkana, Tyler, and Marshall.

The Plan faced many difficulties and only lasted seven years. There were disagreements between the agencies that oversaw the program and issues with integration into the local communities. And while Schiff and his associates back in New York may have had romantic notions about settling people out West, the reality was that the immigrants preferred to move to places with religious significance such as Palestine or with established Jewish communities in this country. Also, the U.S. economy was facing a depression in the early 1900s so job opportunities were not abundant and the small towns were not open to new immigrants taking jobs and adding to social pressures. Altogether the Galveston Plan brought about 10,000 immigrants through the Port of Galveston. Not many in the overall context of the great migration of the period. However, the Galveston Plan was a distinct and largely unknown chapter in the history of Texas.[3]

Louis Williams moved on to Abilene, TX where he and a boyhood friend established the Western Iron and Metal Company, which was some kind of scrap metal business. During the ensuing years he would travel to New York for both business and in pursuit of a proper Jewish wife. He was apparently successful in both endeavors. By 1919 he and his wife, Minnie, had relocated to Detroit, Michigan. Shortly thereafter, he returned to Poland in order to find and bring back family members. Unfortunately, he got caught up in the Polish revolution which occurred at the end of the First World War when Poland attempted to become a free country, and he apparently had some difficulty returning. Eventually, he did manage to get back to his family in Detroit. Minnie used to relate the story that after not hearing from him for months, she feared the worst. He did return, unannounced, gaunt and obviously worn out from his stressful ordeal in evading the Polish forces. However, his appearance at her door was cause for marked celebration.

Meanwhile, Minnie was having health problems as she couldn't take the climate in Detroit. There were cousins in Asheville, NC, so the doctors suggested going to the mountains until she regained her health. Shortly after arriving, her health did improve and they decided to relocate permanently; first to Asheville in 1922 and then to Hendersonville, in 1926. Minnie went on to live to age 92, and she and Louis raised a family of three children, Jakey, Sammy, and Auntie Anne, and I grew up with and knew all three of them, their children, grandchildren, and one great-grandchild (so far).

Louis Williams initially went into the same kind of scrap metal business that he originally knew in Texas, but in 1926 there was a huge land boom (bubble) in Henderson County, NC driven by Florida speculators—according to a history left by his son, Sammy—and he went into real estate. The boom lasted for two years and Mr. Williams, I imagine along with a lot of other people in Hendersonville, apparently became caught up in the thick of it and ended up losing all his money. So, he went back to the junkyard, scrap metal business, where he was once again successful, and by the time of the Depression in the 1930s, he was one of the few businessmen doing well enough that he could give modest loans to those in need.

Uncle Morris, Dad's younger brother, went into the Army during World War II and became good friends with Sammy Williams from Hendersonville. One day, Sammy got a letter from home and, as the story goes, Morris noticed a picture that was enclosed. He said, "So Sammy, who is this pretty girl?" Sammy said, "Why that's my sister, Annie." Uncle Morris said to Sammy, "Hello! My, she's pretty; can I write to her?" And so Sammy, thinking, "Well, here's a nice Jewish boy from Scranton, said "Sure why not." And, so began a beautiful romance. I believe this was either the end of 1943 or sometime early in 1944, because in 1945 when the war ended, Morris came to Hendersonville and married Annie.

Well, that's the version I heard all my life from Uncle Morris. Now, here's another version that I found in the oral history that Sammy recorded sometime before he died:

Interviewer: How did you meet Morris Kaplan?

Sammy: Morris and I were stationed in Madison, Wisconsin. We were at the radio school. And it happened to be one day I was in the barracks there and I was walking down from the barracks and there was this young solider there. He wasn't feeling very well and I went over to him and I asked him, "Is there something I can help you with?" He didn't even know I was Jewish at the time and he said, "Yeah, I feel terrible," and he asked me for some aspirin or cough medicine and I went over and struck up a conversation, discussing where I was from and all, and he found out I was Jewish and we started hanging out together. We had some dates with girls up at the university in Madison. On our days off we'd go up there to different museums and seemed to have a lot in common. So, I told him, I said, "I have a sister." And he said, "You mind if I write her?" And I said, "Go ahead."

Anyway, he must have corresponded with her, I didn't ask too much about it. And as we parted company I said, "If you're ever down my way you have the address and everything, drop in and see us." Sure enough, he got stationed in the South around Virginia. I guess one weekend he decided to drop in and see her. I didn't know what was going on because I was overseas already, but evidently they hit it off pretty well because they got married before I ever got back from service.

By that time, Louis Williams was long settled in Hendersonville and had the family business, Louis Williams and Sons, a hardware store, junkyard, auto-parts, plumbing supply, and most anything else that he could buy and sell to make money and help out the good citizens of Hendersonville and make a living for his family. Louis and his wife, Minnie, and their children welcomed Uncle Morris with open arms into their family, their lives, and into their business. And Morris and Annie raised two chil- dren, my cousins David and Eileen, and lived in Hendersonville for the rest of their lives, some 65 years. So, either version seems to work out to the same ending.

Some call it fate, others call it luck, others just call it life, the way things happen; the accidents. My mother always said that everything was preordained—*besheirt*, in Yiddish. In studying the Torah we study that God gives us free will, and I like to believe that perhaps we have free will, but it's a hard thing to believe that we have total free will when you look at certain chains of life's events. They make you wonder if God sometimes doesn't push things in a certain direction just to see what will happen. After all, why did Louis Williams come to Hendersonville, of all places? This tiny little town stuck away in the wilderness of Western North Carolina. Why did Morris and Sammy happen to team up in the barracks at some Army post? Why did a picture fall out of a letter when Morris happened to be standing there sick and needing a hand? All of these accidents led directly to my growing up in Canton, NC. Any one of them not happening, and I'm a totally different person today.

Because Morris married Annie and found a home in Hendersonville, and Dad was unhappy looking at the future in Scranton and wasn't sure what else to do, Morris apparently encouraged him to come down to Western North Carolina.

But, what was he going do to down there? Dad, after all, had been trained in a yeshiva, an Orthodox Jewish school for the religious and secular education of children of elementary school age. He had really wanted to be a rabbi or at least a teacher, had tried to get into seminary, but instead had gone on to law school and obtained a Juris Doctorate degree, but had never gone before the bar. He decided that he couldn't get a job as a lawyer, or didn't want to. He and Mom apparently had no idea how to go about starting a career, so Morris encouraged him to come down here to Western North Carolina to the wilderness of small-town America to do what exactly?

Louis Williams had a cousin, Sam Kaye, in an even smaller town, further west and deeper into the mountains (what a schlep!) in Murphy, NC. They got together and set Dad up in the auto-parts business in another small town nearby—and that's how we got to Canton, NC.

Molly Pollack Kaplan
Scranton, PA 1939

Joe, Morty & baby Judy
Scranton, PA 1945

Mom & Dad on honeymoon
Miami, FL 1939

Grandma Kaplan & Morty
Scranton, PA 1940

Morty, Mom & Joe
Scranton, PA 1944

Uncle Morris, Aunt Anne & Uncle Bernie at
Morris & Anne's wedding, likely Hendersonville, NC

Canton

A little more history

Canton, NC was founded in 1889 as Buford, then Vinson, and then changed to Pigeon Ford, before settling on its current name of Canton in 1893. Canton was named after the source of the steel from which the bridge was constructed across the Pigeon River, manufactured in Canton, Ohio.

Long before white settlers came to Haywood County and established the town, the area was home to Native Americans. According to the Cherokee myths, just south of Canton the great hunter Kanati and his wife, the great corn maiden Selu, lived in the mountainous forest that is today known as Shining Rock Wilderness Area. The land was rich in wildlife, with fertile soil for farming.

Archaeologists who have studied the Garden Creek site just south of Canton near Bethel estimate that prehistoric human activity took place here as far back as 10,000 years ago. The 12-acre site features two villages that contain three mounds near the Pigeon River. Bone tools, turtle shell rattles, hammer stones, beaded necklaces, river cane mats, clay smoking pipes, shells, and copper have been found in the digs that have taken place there since 1800.

In September 1776, a Colonial army of about 2,500 men marched through the Canton area as part of a preemptive strike against Cherokee towns thought to be in league with the British during the Revolutionary

War. Led by General Griffith Rutherford, the army assembled at Old Fort and marched over the Blue Ridge Mountains along river valleys, crossing the Pigeon River and into Western North Carolina's Cherokee towns where it burned settlements, trampled crops, and confiscated livestock. It would become known as the Rutherford Trace.

Some of the soldiers of that Colonial force later returned to the area to settle and build farms and families. Settlers of German, English, and Scots-Irish ancestry moved into Western North Carolina by the late 1700s and early 1800s. Present-day Canton was once referred to as Pigeon Ford, named after the passenger pigeons that commonly populated the area and were later hunted into extinction. Travelers heading west had to cross the Pigeon River at narrow, shallow segments, so the area would also be known as Ford of Pigeon. By the mid-1800s, a stagecoach service provided limited transportation for passengers, mail, and materials into the area.

Railroad tracks would not be laid to Canton until 1881. With increased access into the mountains by train, more settlers came, and the village of a few houses grew rapidly to include streets with general stores and enterprising merchants. The town flirted with a few names such as Vinson (after a postal clerk) and Buford (after a railroad executive) before settling on the name, Canton, after an iron-truss and steel bridge in town built with metal from Canton, OH. With a name formally approved in 1895, the town of Canton launched into an era of furious building over the next 20 years.

The single most important change to Canton came when Ohio industrialist Peter G. Thomson decided to build a pulp mill in the heart of town in 1906. The massive industry, which cost $2 million to build, $51,282,000 in today's dollars, began operating on January 1, 1908. Construction had been delayed by a shortage of labor, a national economic crisis, and heavy rains that swamped the site. However, within the next few decades, the Champion Paper and Fibre Company would become one of the largest, most productive paper mills of its kind in the world, churning out paper, pulp, chestnut extract, and caustics. More than a century later, it continues, though under a different name and under different ownership.

Arriving in Canton

I don't remember getting there, I just remember being there. I suppose Dad came first. I remember from Mom's stories that she drove down with Uncle Bernie and me, Morty and Judy in Uncle Bernie's 1937 Cadillac LaSalle, and Mom always used to tell us that Uncle Bernie stopped along the road and read every one of the historical markers. She said it drove her crazy, but eventually we arrived. Canton in 1946 was a paper-mill town; a place that smelled really bad. Now, when I say really bad, I mean they physically stink, because a byproduct of making paper is sulfur and sulfur comes out of those smokestacks in huge quantities. In those days, nobody cared about the environment and there were

no filters on the smokestacks and the waste was enormous, and on a bad day the smell was awful. There is a family story that the first morning in Canton, Mom woke up, turned to Dad and said, "Louie, my God, what have you done to me, what is that smell?!"

Our first house in Canton was located at 97 Academy Street. A little brick house which is still there and looks today exactly like it did when we left it in 1952. It is directly across the street from the Baptist church and next door to the Episcopalian church. At the time there was an empty lot on the other side, and next to the empty lot was the Shulman's house. Later, another house was built between us and the Shulmans. In addition to the Shulmans there had been a few other Jewish families in Canton be- fore us. The Winner family had lived there in the 1930s before moving on to Asheville and had a clothing store in Canton; there were one or two others, but we were the only ones who lived and grew up there in the time that we were there. The Shulmans owned the clothing store on Main Street across from Kay's Auto Parts, Dad's store. They had a son and a daughter who were few years older than us; Dickey was the son and I don't remember knowing his older sister. There were three or four Shulman brothers that had similar stores. In addition to the one in Canton, there was a clothing store in Hendersonville, one in Brevard, one in Sylva, and one in Morganton, as well as a very early one in Bryson City. This was typical of Jewish families in the small towns throughout the South of that era.

While the Shulmans were just across the street from us, we had a particularly friendly relationship with his brother, Sol, in Sylva, a town an hour or so west of Canton. We would go there a couple of times a year and load up on clothes for the family. Usually, we would go on a Sunday visit and have lunch—the ubiquitous tuna fish salad and kugels. Sol would open the store just for us. Sol and his wife had two sons, David, who now lives between Asheville and Arizona, with whom I am in contact, and who has helped me with some of this history, and his older brother Herbert. Herbert and I were the same age and good friends. Sadly, he died too young some years ago. There were two other Jewish families in Sylva with kids about our age who I remember, the Karps and the Lessings.

Dad's first store was Kay's Auto Parts on Main Street. From home, it was a short walk down Academy Street, turn left on Main Street, and walk a couple stores down Main to get to it. I don't remember the number on Main Street, but the phone number was 2705. It was a few years until a fifth digit was added and I remember that some people still had party lines in those days. Remember party lines? Remember operators? Remember heavy, black, hard-wired phones with dials? One phone to a house?

It is likely that those of younger generations reading this have no idea what I'm talking about here. Okay, here's a brief explanation and a couple of pictures. In the early days of telephones, especially in rural America, all calls went through a central switchboard run by a real live human, almost always a female operator.

When you picked up the phone, you didn't dial a number, she would answer and place your call. Later, the next advancement was number dialing, but the problem was more than one house would have the same numbers assigned to them so when the phone rang you didn't know if the call was for you or a neighbor. That system was called a party line and you could never be sure if your nosy neighbor was listening in on your calls or not. I think that lasted until the numbers went from three to four digits.

Party lines were common in that period in rural areas where wires had to be run miles to remote homes and shared service meant that more homes could be served with fewer wires. The drawbacks were outweighed by the reduced monthly cost. When you picked up your phone while somebody else on your party line was talking, you'd overhear his or her conversation—and could join in. The shared line meant not only that you could not make a call if somebody else was using the line, but that nobody else could call you. If one person on the party line was using it, anybody trying to call any of the other people on that same line would get a busy signal. Certain people did gain a reputation for being nosy and always trying to listen in on other people's calls to hear the latest gossip, or for always tying up the line with excessively long calls. These things were sometimes noted in movies and television shows of the time, e.g. the running gag in the 1962 movie, Mr. Hobbs Takes A Vacation, where every time somebody picks up the phone the local gossip is always on the line. The 1959 classic movie, Pillow Talk, has a party line as the essential plot feature, with smooth-talking Rock Hudson always tying up the line with sweet-talk to his lady friends, much to the annoyance of Doris Day who could never make or receive a call.

There were a number of variations of precise party-line arrangements used in different places and at different times, and independent phone companies often adopted slightly different methods from the Bell System. The most basic scheme was a two-way party line, and these could be arranged so that each phone would ring only for its own calls. If you picked up when the other person was using the line, you'd jump right in on the conversation, but you wouldn't know when the other person's phone was ringing. Four-way lines could also be wired for fully selective ringing, but many were partially selective, meaning that coded rings were employed. Your phone would ring for your own calls and for those of one of the other parties, and you had to remember whether your assigned ring was a single long ring or two short rings or some combination. In rural areas, 8- and 10-way party lines were not uncommon. These always involved some sort of coded ringing, with various schemes being used; e.g. party 1 might be a single long ring, party 2 would be two short rings, party 3 long-short, party 4 long-short-short, etc. They could be split so that you would hear the coded rings for yourself and some, but not all, of the other parties. Incredibly, there were even 10-way party lines back in the 1940s; it was a cheap way to get telephone service for those who just wanted it for occasional use. Long-distance calls were expensive and something of a special occasion back when even a telegram could be cheaper.

But with the equipment used in some places, particularly those large 10-way arrangements, the numbers could be grouped. Everybody on the same party line would have the same phone number, except for the last digit. So if your number was 2643, the other people sharing your line would be 2641, 2642, 2644, and so on. That made it easy for the equipment to select the line and then just use the last digit to decide which of the coded rings to send out. Anyone who had a private line on those systems had a number ending in 1, and the other nine numbers, which would otherwise share the line, were unused. Back in those days, there were still many places with manual service, meaning that when you picked up a phone, there were no dial telephones, just pick up and wait for the operator to ask, "Number please?" These could have all sorts of different numbering to identify parties, and you might have had to ask for "254 ring 1" or "254 ring 3." Another common arrangement on manual service that catered for up to four parties per line was to use a single letter J, M, R, or W after the number. So if your number was 387-J, the three other people sharing your line were 387-M, 387-R, and 387-W. When anyone asked for a call to any of those numbers, the operator would plug into line 387 and then just press a different key for J, M, R, or W which selected the type of ringing.

And the phones themselves were heavy, black instruments that were hard-wired into the wall and only the telephone repair man was allowed to move or fix or touch them in any way other than to pick up the receiver to speak into it. The telephone company had a monopoly on every aspect of the telephone and the service and you dared not interfere. In fact, the monopoly was so strong that it was even considered illegal, against the law, to touch the wires or try to fix anything yourself. People were physically afraid of "Ole Ma Bell."

Long distance was another big deal that required operator assistance. Even calling from Canton to Asheville required an operator in the days of four-digit numbers. First we graduated to five numbers and then finally to seven digit exchanges and then the great revolution of area codes. I remember that being extremely revolutionary and controversial. Finally AT&T (also known as The Bell System or Ma Bell) was broken up and you would have thought the world was going to come to an end— now there were colored telephones—designer phones! You didn't need the phone company's permission to buy one! What a revolution it was. It's hard to believe today.

Seven digit phone numbers with area codes didn't come to our part of the country until I was in high school. I don't remember the phone number of the house because I seldom called the house, but we called the store a lot.

The first store

The store was just a little hole-in-the-wall I guess. Even today looking back, as a child I remember it as a little tiny store. I don't think Dad knew much about the auto parts business, but he sure worked hard and his hands were dirty all the time. Dad had great big hands with thick, strong fingers; much different hands and fingers than mine, which are long and thin. His hands were like his mother's; they could make things and do delicate work even though they were so big and strong.

Here is one of those strange coincidences that I talked about a while ago. Mom was trained in high school as a secretary bookkeeper in Scranton. There was a big auto-parts wholesale company in Scranton, and when she got out of high school she went to work for this company as a bookkeeper and she learned the auto-parts business. So, when they went to Canton, I think Mom may have known more about the auto-parts business then Dad did. She certainly knew how to keep the books and she had the most beautiful handwriting of anybody I ever knew. Of course, everything was done by hand except she had a great big multi-key adding machine that she taught me how to use as a little boy.

She kept these great big ledgers and recorded everything using a Schaefer fountain pen, which I still have. Then she'd add up these long columns of figures on this big adding machine which produced a long paper tape. I doubt she ever made a mistake. She'd create columns of figures on the adding machine, rip off the tape and I'd read the numbers to her while she checked them off, or she'd read the numbers and I'd check them off; I don't ever remember one of them being wrong. I loved working in the store, but I suppose if I had to sit in a class in school called bookkeeping, I'd have hated it. I did finally take accounting in graduate school at Wharton Business School of the University of Pennsylvania as an adult. I couldn't believe that there were actually textbooks teaching the things my mother taught me as a little boy. Didn't everybody grow up knowing about ledgers and that the debits had to balance the credits and the difference between an invoice and statement and how to make a bank deposit?

Here's a funny aside. Kay's Auto Parts was called our "store." We'd go to Hendersonville on weekends when Dad and Uncle Morris bought stuff (inventory) together at Louis Williams and Son's Company, which they called the "shop," which sold new and used auto parts, as well being a junk yard, plumbing supply, hardware store, etc. We went on Sundays to Uncle Morris's house and had lunch—more tuna fish salad, kugel, Swiss cheese. The menu never varied. To this day my cousins and I joke about it—then we went down to the "shop" because Louis Williams and Son's Company was the "shop," but Kay's Auto Parts was the "store." Even today, 60 years later, my cousins David and Eileen talk about the "shop" and we talk about the "store." It's to wonder why.

Telephone operators circa 1940

Growing up in Canton

Well, now that you've got that bit of history, let's get on to the rest of the story.

I look back at the years in Canton as having had a good time. I had some good friends, and it's during those years that I discovered books. I read Tom Sawyer, then Huck Finn, and eventually, I read everything else Mark Twain wrote. I think he was the first author that I fell in love with in many ways. Over the years, that has been a pattern of mine. From the time I first learned to read, I don't think I've ever been without a book in my hand, beside my chair or my bed. I would find an author that I liked and go on a binge of reading everything they published. I related to Tom and Huck because growing up in Canton, I felt like I had that same kind of freedom they experienced.

From age 8 till 13, we were free. We ran around barefoot and shirtless all summer long. Not only were we allowed to run free, some of my friends' mothers literally locked them out of the house telling them, "Don't come back till dinner time." How did we know when dinner was? No one had a watch, but we were seldom ever late, we always seemed to know when it was time to be home. Sometimes we would hear a mother yelling somebody's name from her front or back porch suggesting that it was time for someone to go home.

I remember racing home the last day of school kicking off shoes, socks, and shirts, and putting on shorts and that's all I wore for the rest of summer. Our feet would hurt until we got used to it, toughening them on the hard ground and the rocks and the street. Imagine a pack of rough little boys running freely over the hills and the countryside, splashing through muddy streams, climbing over or under fences. Maybe chasing, or more likely, running from a cow in a field. Making up our own games and entertaining ourselves playing cowboys and Indians or a game of softball or football. Running in and out of someone's home for a snack, milk and cookies maybe. Riding bikes. Totally free of any adult supervision, but knowing that there were limits without ever thinking about it or being told because everyone knew who we were. I don't ever recall doing anything malicious or destructive except on those times when it was more or less expected, that is, Halloween or Fourth of July when a little bad behavior was acceptable.

Every night I would get into the tub with filthy feet and feel good about seeing how dirty I could make the water. Aren't little boys wonderful? By the end of the summer, we all had nice dark tans. We wandered in small gangs of four, five, or six tough little boys all over the hills around Canton getting into minor scrapes, falling, fighting, and bicycling. We played pickup baseball games, made slingshots, corncob pipes, and smoked corn silks. Of course, what would summer be without skinny-dipping in the river?

Let me tell you how to make a corncob pipe. In the fall, after the corn was harvested, we'd walk through a corn field looking for unharvested heads of corn, which either hadn't been picked or had fallen to the ground and left there. You'd find a likely candidate and shuck it—peel away all the husk down to the corn which was probably pretty well dried out by then. Next, you take out your trusty pocket knife. Yes, any self-respecting 12-year-old in those days carried an all-purpose pocket knife. After all, you never knew when you'd find a good stick that needed some whittlin'. Or in this case, a corn cob that you had to scrape all the dried corn off of.

Or to play a game of mumblety-peg (more on that later). After scraping all the corn off the cob, you decide just how long you want the barrel of your pipe to be and cut a length of cob from the bottom till it's two or three inches long. That's the barrel of the pipe. Next, you have to hollow out—"holler' out," in the local vernacular—the inside of the cob making a bowl, usually using the second, smaller blade on your knife. When this is done you have to make a hole near the bottom for the stem to go in.

You may be wondering just where is the stem is going to come from? Well, as you may imagine, every good corn field needs to be watered, so they were usually planted near a stream or a creek—pronounced, *crick*. And growing on the banks of almost any creek in these-here parts, you'll find a pretty good stand of bamboo. Bamboo is neat stuff to play with and we found all sorts of things to do with it and the only tools you needed were your trusty pocket knife and maybe some matches because bamboo is easy to work.

For the pipe stem we needed to find a nice piece of bamboo about a quarter inch in diameter and four or five inches long, which was easy to cut off a plant down on the creek. Bamboo grows in a unique way in that every six or so inches, it makes a solid knot and then a new hollow growth begins again so it had to be cut between the knots and you would have a nice hollow pipe the length needed. Except, there was still a problem. You may have noticed I referred to needing matches, and, oh yes, a wire coat hanger came in handy as well. While mother nature thoughtfully provided us with this nice hollow pipe, it was a living thing that wasn't totally hollow inside. Stuff grew in there. A kind of pulp that had to be removed to finally have a clean, clear pipe that you could actually use for smoking; or maybe to use as a blow gun to shoot small seeds or BBs through. As I said, bamboo had many uses.

The next stage was to light a small fire—we were all Boy Scouts by then and knew how to do such things—get a wire coat hanger, heat the coat hanger until it was red hot and ram it inside the bamboo stick, thus burning out the pulp and anything that was inside our evolving pipestem. It worked like a charm except for the obvious danger which led to various minor cuts and burns. Now, it was just a matter of trimming the ends and fitting the stem into the hole at the bottom of the corn cob and voila—a corn cob pipe.

What did we smoke in our newly manufactured corn cob pipes? Occasionally we would take a cigarette apart and smoke tobacco or someone would get hold of some actual Prince Albert-in-a-can pipe tobacco, but since we were in a corn field, the most abundant crop was left over dried out corn silks. Not bad as I recall. And, yes, my mother found a pipe left in a pocket more than once.

Canton was a small town—a country town where some of my friends lived on farms. Their parents or grandparents had farms that grew tobacco mostly. Nobody worried about any of the things that we worry about today, so I had fun growing up and I did things that I doubt my mother ever knew about, except when I fell down hurt myself and came crying home a bloody mess. Our group included me and my friends Buddy and Terry, Mark, Tommy, Billy, Becky, Betty Lou, (she broke Morty's arm once) and Jerry to name a few.

We kept track of the stitches we would get when we got hurt falling down or getting into a fight. Whoever had the most stitches wore an invisible badge of honor for the summer. I had a lot of stitches, as I was tall and clumsy and skinny; I had stitches in my hands, in my legs, over my eye, and around my ear. I forget now how many I had then, but I had a lot of stitches and some of the scars are still visible. Luckily, I didn't have any broken bones even after falling and sliding all the way down the old rock quarry where we were never supposed to be playing. This old rock quarry was much too attractive a place to stay away from. Today they make these artificial places where they teach kids rock climbing with ropes and harnesses and such, but this was the real thing without any of that stuff, including adult supervision. We figured out our own ways of climbing up and down the face of the rocks and knew where the hand and foot holds were. I don't know how high it was but it was pretty much vertical with some paths to follow. One time I was almost at the top when my foot slipped and lost my grip and slid all the way to the bottom. Everything—hands, elbows, knees, feet, nose, forehead, stomach—was scraped and bleeding by the time I got to the bottom. Nothing bad enough for more stitches and nothing broken, but plenty of tears and sorrowful explanations.

Speaking of tobacco farms, one year sometime in the middle of my grammar school years, it was announced that there would be a Christmas pageant, as was typical each year. Well, a couple of my buddies and I desperately did not want anything to do with being in the Christmas pageant and would do anything to get out of it. So, we came up with a plan. The family of one of the guys had a tobacco farm not too far out of town. In fact, it was within bicycle distance and we used to ride out there fairly regularly in the summer time. I suppose it was three or four, maybe five miles. His grandfather had a lot of neat stuff that he liked to show us such as a display case with old documents, which I believe were things like the family's original land grant. There were also old rifles on the walls and above the stone fireplace.

The main crop, like in so much of the area, was tobacco, and he would explain to us how it was grown, harvested, and dried. He showed us how the huge leaves were tied in bundles and hung from the rafters in the special barn which didn't have sides so the air could circulate and dry out the tobacco leaves. When you looked up, you'd see row after row of drying tobacco. He also taught us what twist was. And now, we come to the point of the story. He showed us how he would take a few leaves and twist them very tightly together, then tie them with twine in a small bundle and set them out to dry for a long time. Eventually, they would dry out enough to make an especially strong—and desirable, if you were a real aficionado (although no one around there would ever use that word)—chewing tobacco (*chawin' bacc'r*). You really had to be a professional, experienced tobacco chewer to use that stuff, believe me! Of course, we little kids didn't know that at the time and our plan was just to get hold of some. We just knew that it was pretty strong stuff. It was suggested that we chop off a chunk of Grampa's twist— unbeknownst to him of course—again using our trusty pocket knives, and on the morning of the pageant we would each put a bit in our mouths, chew it, and get just a little bit sick; enough to skip the pageant.

To say we got sick doesn't begin to do the story justice. I don't believe any of us had ever chewed tobacco before and didn't know about the all-important, spitting-out part. We certainly had observed men chewing and spitting, but somehow had never figured out or thought about the rhythm of it, and without any experience and no notion of how fast tobacco juice is created in your mouth, one swallow was all it took, and we were falling out of our seats and rolling on the floor in agony and the teacher was calling the janitor to come clean up the mess. Needless to say, we accomplished our mission.

Other memories of growing up in Canton centered around working in Dad's store. I loved working in the store. Dad got up early, probably around six or seven, and the store was walking distance from our house, so he'd walk to work. Again, it was a really small town, less than 5,000 people I'd guess. The surrounding county was covered with farms. Tobacco farms and truck farming, which is defined as farming vegetables. A lot of trucks broke down and Dad fixed them. Mom got us off to school; she would always make us lunches made of peanut butter and jelly or cream cheese and jelly or tuna fish sandwiches. We walked to school with a lot of other neighbor kids. Some would come to school barefoot and some came on the bus from out in the country. I expect there were some that were hungry, and of course, schools were segregated so they were, looking back, interesting times. There were no black kids in our school and I have no idea how many black people even lived in Canton or Haywood County at the time. There was a Cherokee Indian population, as we lived near the reservation. So, we also saw mixed black and Cherokee people; these were descendants of those who had avoided the forced move west in the nineteenth century. We were never taught any of that history, except when we went to the Cherokee Reservation and saw the famous play, Unto These Hills, that is still being presented there today. It portrays how badly the Cherokee people were treated.

I met with a couple of the girls I grew up with for an interview for this book, and we talked for a couple of hours. One of the things we talked about was race and race relations in Canton. They reminded me about the Negro high school, The Reynolds School and pointed me to a book, one in a series, called Images of America, CANTON, by Michael Beadle. There is a picture of the graduating class of 1955 which consisted of 12 students. The Reynolds School was finally integrated into the Haywood County system when the new high school was built in 1966. I was only vaguely aware that the school or those kids even existed in Canton.

I do have one, very distinct memory, however, of a racial awakening or consciousness. One of my motivations for writing this book is a response to a questions that I have always been asked about anti-Semitism in such a small southern town as Canton. One my first rejoinders has always been to inform the person that, first of all, there is a difference between the South, and the Appalachian Mountains; or at least I always felt that way. Certainly, the accents and the language is unique if you pay attention. There is a substantial difference between where I grew up and, say, the Low Country of South Carolina or Alabama or Mississippi.

The point I want to get to is that while everyone was concerned about our relations as Jews, the real problems were the problems of segregation of blacks and whites, even with the limited black population that existed in Canton. I distinctly remember the public water fountain on Main Street with the sign engraved on it that said whites only and the bus station with the whites only waiting rooms in both Canton and Asheville. One of the women whom I interviewed told me about her father's irrational hatred of all black people, even though she could never remember him ever having relationships with anyone other than white people. To this day, she has no idea where the hatred came from.

The personal story I want to tell happened when I was 12 or 13 and Dad employed one of the few black men in town as a mechanic to do whatever needed doing around the store. Across the street and down the block a short distance was Charlie's Café, a small diner where I would go occasionally for a sandwich or a Coke or a snack. One day, I casually asked this fellow if he would like to come with me for some lunch. He gave me this peculiar look that I didn't understand and said no, he couldn't go. I asked what he meant by, "He couldn't go." Embarrassed by my question I guess, he was forced to explain to me that he wasn't allowed to go in the front door and sit down at the counter or a table and eat lunch. If he wanted something to eat, he had to go around to the back door and knock, and hope the owner would come and sell him something, which he regularly refused to do.

I remember being totally amazed, confused, and I guess embarrassed at this and walked away. I don't recall if I discussed it with my parents or not, but never forgot it. This was well before the phrase "civil rights" became part of anyone's vocabulary, but a few years later when the first sit-ins started to occur at lunch counters, I thought of that incident and I wondered if that man had the courage to sit at Charlie's Café in Canton, and what the people of Canton did. I don't know how integration happened in

Canton—quietly, successfully, or violently, but I my guess is, it just sort of happened without a lot of fuss and bother with only a few hot-heads spewing hatred, and the town fathers keeping the lid on.

    I realize in looking back that, while we lived in Canton, we were not of Canton. We lived in Canton, went to school there, Dad had a successful auto parts business there, participated in civic affairs, had friends in the community, and I was a Boy Scout and played JV basketball in that town. Even so, we were separate from the social fabric of the community in some ways. In thinking about writing this book and reflecting on my life in Canton, I have come to realize that I did not really know any of the people that I went to school with, that they had lives that I knew nothing about. Mostly, their lives revolved around their churches and for many of them, if their father worked in the mill, their lives were somewhat circumscribed by where they stood in the pecking order of the mill workers. We knew nothing about any of that. Llewellyn, my school friend, told me that in high school there were two girl's clubs. One was for the girls whose fathers were executives and managers at the mill plus the doctors and lawyers and bankers in town, and the other club was for everyone else and the lines weren't crossed. Who knew that in such a small town there was such a social stratification?

    I need to clarify here that when I refer to the mill I am referring to The Champion Paper and Fibre Company which was the paper mill or simply the mill, which was the life-blood of Canton and the economic reason for Canton's existence.

    The boys all went off and played ball, which is a much more egalitarian social situation. Either you're good enough to make the team or you're not, doesn't matter too much who your father is, although I'm not naïve enough to believe that if your father owns the mill and you want to be on the football team you won't have any trouble making the team. But, in most cases, if you have the talent you play, and if you don't, you don't.

The other thing my siblings and I knew nothing about was the life that revolved around the mill. Of course we knew about the mill, you couldn't miss it. It smelled all the time. It either smelled bad, or it smelled worse, or it was unbearable. And in the summer everyone got the itches, large, red welts that would appear on your skin that itched like crazy. I'm sure the itches were from the pollution from the mill.

If your father worked at the mill, you had a free membership at the YMCA. I got to enjoy the Y once a week on Monday nights after Boy Scouts when we'd go swimming for an hour.

Men swam naked and Monday night was men's night, but at whatever hour was reserved for the scouts, the men left and it was only us boys in this huge indoor pool in the basement of the Y. We then all walked, yes, walked home, at night in the dark; no one would even think of coming to get us and we were happier and better for it. That's one of the brightest examples of what I mean when I say we grew up free.

My friend Llewellyn also told me that her social life up through high school pretty much revolved around the Y. Every day after school there were activity there for the kids. At age five or six there was tap dancing and ballet lessons, (even for her brothers, she said). Then there were sports teams of every sort. However, the girls weren't allowed to walk home alone. They had to wait for a parent or older brother to either walk with them or drive them home.

The Y was open to paid membership to anyone in town, but free to the mill employees. Membership couldn't have cost very much and I wonder why my parents didn't take advantage. I suppose it was that whole problem of not wanting us to get too close to non-Jewish girls. The only other activity I remember doing there was, at some point, Mom decided that I needed to learn to dance and they had dancing classes. I suppose Morty was included, but I don't recall. Learning to dance was about as successful as all my other musical endeavors. Let's just say that there won't be a chapter titled Musical Accomplishments. The one thing I learned from that experience was how good it felt to hold a girl's hand and how good my hands smelled afterward! There was soap or perfume or bath water or something that rubbed off onto my hands that had a sweet odor that I will never forget. But, I was already head and shoulders above all these tiny little girls, had no sense of rhythm or movement, was stiff as board, and had big feet that kept going places other than where they were intended to land. I don't think anyone really wanted me as a dance partner.

Mumblety Peg

Mumblety Peg is one of the little boy games that we played that we never wanted our mothers to know about. It involved little sticks and knives. There are a couple of others I ought to include here that were equally as dumb, which added matches and clothespins, BB guns, and slingshots.

I looked it up and discovered that there are variations on this game that have a history going back into the nineteenth century. I actually learned to play Mumblety Peg in the Boy Scouts. The version we played went something like this: Two boys would stand opposite each other, feet apart. The first player takes his pocket knife—see, I keep emphasizing how important pocket knives are for little boys—throws it at the ground so that it sticks into the ground as close as possible to his own foot. The second player does the same thing. The player who comes closest to his foot wins. If you stick the knife in your own foot you automatically win. Winning means you take a short stick, pound it into the ground, and your opponent has to dig it out with his teeth.

There are other versions where you throw the knife at each other's feet or you don't throw at feet but at the ground with various kinds of trick tosses. Mark Twain has Tom Sawyer playing the game.

Matches and clothes pins

We had another favorite sport which was making clothespin match guns. These used two things that you don't see much of in today's world. One being clothespins. Big, heavy, wooden clothespins with tight, steel springs. The other being wooden matches, what were called Strike Anywhere Matches—I am certain they are the reason safety matches were invented. I don't know who dreamed this up, but someone figured out how to combine matches and clothes pins into a fine little mechanism to shoot lighted matches at each other. I'll try to describe how it worked.

First, you take the clothespin apart so that you have three pieces. Then you take out your pocket knife and carve the wooden parts of the clothespin in a way that I have forgotten so when you reattach the spring it acts as a trigger. Now, you get a box of those big wooden matches and break off the head, leaving about an eighth of an inch of stick below the head. Taking another complete clothespin, you take the re-manufactured clothespin and slip it into the whole clothespin with the match head and hold it like a gun. When you pull the spring/trigger it will strike the match head, light it and send it flying a few feet, burning brightly. We had the greatest fun shooting these things at each other. My mother could never figure out what those strange brown spots were on my tee shirts!

I've tried to figure out how these were made but completely forgotten exactly how to cut the clothespin to fit the spring. It's a lost art. Maybe someone will read this and remember. Hopefully not.

Working in the store

As we got older, after school I would go to the store instead of going home. As I said, the store was just down the street and around the corner from home and Mom worked in the store with Dad. She did the books at her desk in a little corner behind the counter. The first store was pretty small. I suppose it wasn't more than maybe 15 feet across the front and 15 or 20 feet deep. You walked in a double front door and there was a counter across the front that was four or so feet high and six or eight feet long. On the counter were the books, the great big catalogues, with all the auto parts listed so you could look up the parts when somebody came in and said they wanted such and such a part for such and such a model car. You had to know how to look it up. Dad taught me how to do this very early on, and it was a skill that served me well years later in college when I went to work for another parts dealer.

Another skill that I learned working in the store from the time I was little, maybe 10 or 12 years old, was how to read numbers. I learned later in life, when I was in college and then in the Army, that people don't know how to attack a large, multi-digit number. Dad showed me how to break it down into smaller numbers—three- or four-digit sets—so it then becomes much easier to see and to read. The reason it was important is that auto parts all have very long numbers—8, 10, 12, or 16 digits. When you have an auto parts store, you have to take inventory more than once a year, maybe quarterly or semiannually. Taking inventory is a sizable job and that was one of the early, serious things that dad taught us to do to help in the store.

There were two jobs in taking inventory. One was to call out the numbers and the quantity of parts and the other was to write down the numbers in long columns on the pages of inventory sheets. It was important to know how to read a 10- or 12-digit number by breaking it down. Because reading all those digits one at a time becomes very tedious and it is easy to make mistakes both in reading and writing.

It was a skill I learned at a very young age and which I've remembered and used my whole life. Later, when I was in basic training in the Army, there were three numbers we had to learn before we were allowed into the mess hall for our first meal: We had to be able to recite our Social Security number, our military ID number, and the serial number of our rifle. I knew my Social Security number, and the other two numbers were also 10- or 12-digit numbers. It took me about five minutes to learn them and remember them because I knew how to break them down. So I showed the guys around me how to do it, what the trick was. The guys who were struggling to remember these long strings of numbers, which is an almost impossible task, were able to master it quickly. For instance, my military ID was (still is, I guess 13816187). When I was told to memorize it instead of seeing those eight digits I saw three numbers: 13 816 187. I've never forgotten it. Three numbers are easier to remember than a string of eight digits. In fact when I look at the whole string I see them jumping around and hard to focus on. I have to admit I haven't a clue what my rifle number was. Whenever I see a long string of numbers I look for sets of two or three, sometimes four as in the last four digits of the social security number. I recently took a course on the history of numbers and learned that our brain typically can't handle longer sets than three or four.

 I can still picture the way the store looked. Behind the counter there were shelves with rows of auto parts. In the first little store, I recall there were four rows of shelves and additional shelves on each side wall. In the front, on either side of the front door, there were two big picture windows looking out onto the street and there were displays of merchandise on the floor under the windows. It was only a couple steps from the front door to the counter, so not much space for displays on the floor in front of the counter, but there were a couple of stools for customers to sit on while they were being helped. Nevertheless there were usually stacks of merchandise, perhaps cases of motor oil or bags of tire chains in the winter or antifreeze. On the walls were displays of tools, screw drivers, and wrenches and different sorts of mechanics tools.

 In those days all cars had flat, clear glass windows that could easily be cut from large sheets of glass, so Dad got into the glass-cutting business.

He bought this large table with a clear plastic top. Inside was a huge roll of paper with the outlined pattern of every glass window of every car made up the early 1950s. When someone needed a new window for a car he would look up the window: Perhaps a front driver's side window for a 1948 Chevrolet four-door sedan or a little vent window for '37 Ford, and he would get a part number. Then he would scroll through the table until he found that window, take out a piece of glass from his stock, lay it over the pattern, and with a glass cutting tool, score the glass following the outline from the pattern. One of the clever and also difficult things about this was that the patterns intertwined with each other so he had to figure out exactly which pattern he was working with.

This was very hard, intense work. I know, I tried it and could never get it right. The glass was two-piece safety glass with a plastic material in between, so after it was scored with the cutter on both sides, it had to be heated and then carefully broken out of the larger piece. He put lighter fluid on it, lit it, melted the plastic layer and bent and sliced away the window. Now you had the window with very dangerous, sharp edges. So the next step was to sand the glass edges on an upright belt sander which took about half an hour.

Dad got very good at this and it was a great business for a number of years until curved windshields with all kinds of fancy, tinted glass came out and that was the end of that. He tried buying pre-made windows for re-sale but the margins weren't worth the efforts. He once explained the profit in that glass business: There was a list price that he tried to sell a window for, but if he gave a 50% discount and then was really generous and gave an additional 25% discount, he still doubled his money on the cost of the glass! The glass was dirt cheap, he did all the work himself, and there was no other cost involved. He tried to teach other people to do it, but it was very exacting work, and if there was too much waste all that great profit went into the trash can. I eventually got to the point I could almost do it most of the time, but only he had the really steady hand. Besides, he really loved doing that sort of thing.

This was all taking place in the late 1940s, 1946-1950, when I was eight or nine years old. The first completely redesigned post-war car produced by one of the Big Three (GM, Ford, Chrysler) was the 1949 Ford, which came out in June of 1948.

We were way back up in the mountains, about as rural as you could get, where nobody had any money to buy anything new and nobody threw anything away, so people were fixing old cars and farmers fixed their old trucks, tractors, and farm equipment. They would bring in parts from cars and other vehicles they needed to fix—a starter or a generator or carburetor or a whole engine. Sometimes they'd bring the motor from one vehicle in the back of a truck.

Occasionally, the car would break down in front of the store or nearby, as that was far as it would get. Dad and maybe a part-time mechanic would just fix the car out there on the street and nobody bothered them. I only have the vaguest memory of that; Morty told me stories about that.

But, I'll tell you what I do remember. I remember Dad had a black guy, a Negro guy, as we said then, working for him. I don't remember his name, but I remember him being a friendly guy and a huge, strong man. We didn't have a mechanical lift of any kind in the store at that time, but this guy could pick up an engine. He'd just wrap his arms around it and pick it up. He'd say, "Mr. Kay, where y'all want me to put it?" And he would move it to where dad needed it. The store was called Kay's Auto-Parts: K-A-Y-s. So Dad was known as Mr. Kay, or just "Kay" to everybody in town. The store, the business, was named Kay's Auto Parts because Sam Kaye (with an "e" on the end, who was Louis William's cousin, helped Dad get started plus, I always assumed, Kay was easier for the locals to learn than "Kaplan." Believe it or not, the local people had a great deal of trouble with Kaplan for reasons I never could understand. The variations of spelling and permutations of pronunciations just boggle the mind for what seems to be a fairly straightforward, phonetic word. Even the teachers in school had trouble with it. Somehow the letter "k" just became unpronounceable.

Dad would sell just about anything having to do with a car and I learned the names of all the parts. I think that by the time I was 10 or 12, I knew everything there was to know about those simple engines. I could tell the difference between a piston from a Ford, a Chevrolet, and a Plymouth just by looking at them. I knew the basic principle of an internal combustion engine and how and why it worked and how all the parts worked together. I knew why the motor started when you pushed the starter button. And I learned where not to put your fingers when the mechanic was working on the engine.

Another thing I learned at a very early age was that when the phone rang, you answered it because somebody might want to buy something and that's what put food on our table. When we had our bigger store in Asheville, we had men working for us behind the counter. They'd stand around talking and smoking their pipes. I can still remember this one guy, Brownie, who also drank a bit too much, and he let that damn phone ring and ring. I'd look over at him because it was his job to answer it, and he just let it ring. I couldn't stand it, so if it rang more than twice, I'd grab the phone. As a result, I've had a phone fetish my entire life. To this day, I never let the phone ring more than once because it might be somebody who wants to buy something. I've worked in real estate offices where they'd let the phone ring and it drove me crazy. I'd go to answer it and get yelled at because it wasn't my up! "But the phone's ringing! Somebody wants to buy a house!"

Another lesson I learned at a very early age working in the store was how to build a sale. When somebody came into the store, you asked if you could help him. He would say, yeah, he needed a certain part for a car or truck. So you'd look it up, go in the back to find it, put it on the counter, and tell him how much it was. He would say okay—but that wasn't the end of the story. If you made a suggestion and said something like, "By the way, you ought to buy . . ." or, "Don't you need . . ." or, "How about a new wrench?" or, "We have screwdrivers on sale. . . " or, "Could you use five pounds of rags?" or any number of things; people would buy stuff! So a $5 sale might become a $10 sale. What he came in for might have a 5% profit while all this other stuff might have a 100% profit, and that's how you make money. If you don't ask, they don't know, and you don't make a sale.

From a very early age I learned the concept of asking for the order. The related concept that I learned was asking for the money. I've observed all my life in sales that there are two concepts that a lot of people have trouble with: one is closing— that is, asking for the order—and the other is asking to get paid, asking for the money, which is even more difficult. When you're standing across the counter from someone and you give him the merchandise and hand him the invoice, it's really not much of a leap to ask, are you paying by cash or check? There were no credit cards in those days, so the only choice was cash or check. Some people had credit, but you had to be careful to whom you extended credit, because you didn't know if you ever going to get paid. That's how I learned to ask for the money.

About my grandfather

Let me tell you a story about my paternal grandfather, Hyman a.k.a. Jeremiah Kaplan. He had made a modest living in Scranton, PA before the Great Depression and World War II remodeling houses, specializing as a house painter and paperhanger. But, he had a big problem; everything had to be done to his specifications, he was always right, and he had a temper—

so I've been told. This temperamental trait, this sense of self-righteousness runs in the family and lives on in the current generation, present company only lightly affected. He died when I was 13 years old, so I never really knew him, except as a child remembers his Grampa, in mostly affectionate terms.

When my father was a boy he used to go out and help his father, often recounting this favorite story. One time, Grampa was negotiating with a lady who wanted him to remodel her kitchen. Everything was going along smoothly until it came to painting the kitchen. In Grampa's professional opinion, all kitchens were yellow. Just as Henry Ford was famous for having said he would build cars any color you wanted as long as it was black, Grampa would only paint kitchens yellow. The lady didn't want a yellow kitchen and a fight ensued. Grampa wouldn't budge, so, needless to say, he didn't get the job. Dad always swore it was a true story, and certainly typifies a family trait that any cousin would recognize in the personalities of many of our uncles and cousins.

Leaving Academy Street

When Alan was born on March 31, 1947 (we always teased him about just missing being a "you know what," April 1 otherwise known as April Fool's day) we were then up to six of us living in the little house on Academy Street. At some point Dad did the Kaplan thing, which was to remodel and enlarge the house. As I recall, he added a bedroom and a bathroom making it into a small three-bedroom/two-bath from an even smaller two-bedroom/one-bath. In addition, he put a red brick façade on the outside and built on a front porch with steps up the hill from the street, all of which remains exactly as it was when it

was finished in about 1950. Remember my story about counting stitches? Here's an account of the first five. The remodel job included new gutters all around the house. Naturally, nice metal gutters laying all over the yard were just the thing for little boys to be running around, and predictably, I fell; or more likely tripped, as I quite naturally tripped over everything. And so, I sliced my hand at the base of my left thumb—five stitches. The scar is still visible.

My grandfather and Uncle Bernie did most of the work as I recall. There is a retaining wall at the street with a cement front where you can still see the pattern of the trowel work of either Grampa or Uncle Bernie. I remember watching him working the trowel and showing me how to use the trowel to leave a deliberate pattern in the finish.

I should note here that my grandparents—Dad's parents— and Uncle Bernie moved to Asheville from Scranton a couple of years after we moved to Canton in 1949 or 1950. They weren't living with us when they worked on the houses. They bought a house in Asheville on Austin Avenue which, naturally, they remodeled, and lived there while they worked on our houses. First doing the house on Academy Street and later the work on the second house on Pisgah Drive.

Moving to Pisgah Drive

Soon, in typical fashion, Mom and Dad decided the house was too small after all and we should move into something bigger. Dad found a house on the corner of Pisgah Drive and Johnson Street, on the other side of the mountain from Penn Avenue School. Now we would have a steeper climb to walk up to school, although it must have been sixth or seventh grade by the time we moved, so the longer walk up the steeper hill wouldn't be my problem much longer. That would be left to Judy and Alan.

We sold the house on Academy Street in 1952 and bought an old, two-story, three-bedroom house on Pisgah Drive, which is still the main, two-lane highway out of town that takes you from Canton to the top of Mount Pisgah. It is a beautiful drive through the country, if you like two-lane country roads and a steep ride up the mountain consisting of sharp switchbacks. I traveled it recently and it hasn't changed in all these years.

Uncle Bernie and Grampa completely gutted the house, rebuilt it, and turned it into a four-bedroom dwelling so that Morty and I shared a room, Judy and Alan each had their own room, and there was a master bedroom for Mom and Dad. Thinking about it now, the term "master bedroom" really isn't what it means today. There was just one bathroom upstairs for all of us as I don't recall there being a bathroom as part of their bedroom. Maybe that's why they got up so early in the morning. There was a second bathroom downstairs.

When the house on Pisgah Drive was finally finished, we went to either Charlotte or Atlanta to buy carpet at some big carpet dealer. Dad, like his father, had to have a discount deal and the best way to get a deal was to cover the floors of the entire house with the same carpet. The fact that Mom may have wanted to decorate the house with a little variety never entered into the negotiation. Dad bought a huge roll of carpet and installed it throughout the entire house—the living room, dining room, den, and bedrooms were all covered with the same carpet. It happened to be a nice color green carpet, but a little variety couldn't have made that much difference. I'm not even sure his issue was in spending the money so much as not having to make decisions.

I don't remember how long it took to do the job, but it seemed like forever. At one point during the renovation there was a wonderful mound of dirt in the front just high enough so we could jump out of the second story window and land on top of it. It seems like it was the typical hard red clay of the area so that when we jumped we sort "thumped" onto it, landed, and rolled so that we got good and dirty. There was no real point to it: just run back in the house, up the stairs, yelling at each other, getting in the way, falling over building materials. Naturally we got yelled at that we were sure to break something or land on a nail or in some way cause grievous bodily injury. But the dirt felt so good and what self-respecting little boy could resist the temptation of jumping out of a second story window? That's the kind of freedom to explore and experiment that made mothers happy and gave us great childhood memories. Maybe in modern psychological parlance it gave us ownership of the place, it made us part of the process, that it was our house.

The downstairs consisted of a living room, dining room, foyer, small den—which became our television room when we finally got one—a large eat-in kitchen and even separate laundry room, and a small bathroom. There was also a playroom almost big enough for a Ping-Pong table if you didn't move around much. We barely squeezed into that playroom, and it was much better suited for model trains and other fun and games needing less room to run around. I think it must have been a pretty luxurious house for Canton at that time. It was a comfortable house, and for the five or six years we lived there, I remember it with great fondness. There were many cold or rainy days when the house was full of our friends who gathered in the large foyer to play games. We actually invented a football game that we could play on our knees using one of the small, six inch toy footballs. The "field" was the distance from the front door down the hall past the dining room to the entrance to the kitchen. I can't believe we had more than two to a side, maybe three. It could get rough and end up with carpet burns on knees and elbows. There were day long Monopoly games, card games, all kinds of ways to entertain ourselves without parents, without television, without computers. Why, sometimes we would even just sit around and talk to each other.

Blinking light

And so, we moved into a nicer, bigger house in a better part of town where we lived for another five years until we moved to Asheville. Pisgah Dr. is also known as Route 110 and runs out of Canton. As you leave Canton the road makes a sharp right turn where the house still stands on the left, still painted the same green and white with the same driveway demanding a dangerous left turn across the highway to enter.

There was a yellow blinking light at the point on route 110 at a somewhat complicated intersection where you can turn four different ways; but it isn't a neat intersection warranting a complete traffic light. It was always a rural route without much traffic. The real problem was that the light blinked yellow night and day, being especially bothersome for those trying to sleep against its constant flashing. Our house faced Pisgah Drive, so one side faced the blinking light around the corner. Upstairs on that side was a bedroom—you guessed it, my bedroom. Now don't get me wrong, it was a very nice bedroom with its share of the aforementioned green carpet, twin beds, shared dresser, desks, lights, cowboy wallpaper, and everything two brothers could want in a bedroom. To atone for the sin of being born second—and taller—I was given the bed against the far wall opposite the window, and there was NO WAY to block that blinking light. Mort—showing true, big-brotherly love—adamantly refused the thought of blackout curtains as he, naturally, could not possibly sleep in total darkness. And so, I suffered, hypnotized and made berserk, subjected to that blinking light every night for five years. Oh, the havoc I unleashed on that light in my mind, lying in my bed: Shotguns, 22s, BB guns, sling shots, dynamite, wire cutters; you name it, even prayers for an accident to take it out. We moved away before that light was changed.

Living in the new house had its advantages. Johnson Street was a short, dead-end street full of kids about the same age as we were, and we were soon all acquainted, running in and out of each others' homes as though we had known each other all of our lives. There were at least three kids named Billy, a Doug, Becky, and four or five others. Then there was the parallel street across the creek, cleverly called Johnson Drive (those Johnsons were great developers) and a few more blocks of an area still known as Highland Park, full of kids.

On warm summer nights we would gather and play out under the street lights without any adult supervision, making up our own version of games such as Kick the Can, Red Light Green Light, and of course the old perennial Hide and Go Seek. I wonder if kids today have any idea what any of those games are, but we played until it was too dark to see and wore ourselves out.

There were girls living over on Johnson Drive, and as we got a little older we started gravitating to Leanna's house where we hung around under the street light in front of her house and talked and visited and began to learn the early stages of the pleasures of being around girls as well as hanging out being one of the guys. This is another wonderful example of what it means to me to grow up free. Children today have no concept of the kind of freedom we had in that place in that time. Parents weren't obsessed over safety, there were no cell phones, everyone knew everyone's kids and looked out for each other. Most of the families went to the same churches and the kids understood discipline—what would happen if we stepped out of line. We were free to run around, make our own rules, live our own lives, explore life, and live with the consequences. We knew that if you fell down you'd get hurt, but someone was there to pick you up. You knew that some kids could run faster or hit the ball further. Some always won, some rarely won. Some got picked first and some weren't wanted on the team. We learned to deal with all that. We knew who the good athletes were who made the first string, and even if you weren't one of them you could still be friends. It never occurred to anyone that an award or trophy should go to anybody except the ones who came in 1st, 2nd, and 3rd. Those were the rules.

That was life, whether it was sports, academics, or jobs. Some families were rich, some were poor. Some kids got Polio and lived in an iron lung, most didn't. Sometimes you got into a fight with another kid and got knocked down, sometimes you did the knocking down. The next day you were helping each other with your homework. Nobody tattled on anybody, and we were still friends. We'd get into knock-down, drag-out, roll-around-in-the-dirt fights, earn black eyes and bruises and forget about it all by the next day. We were free to be ourselves and learn about life. We had fun growing up.

Then, there was the dam. A creek flowed behind our house. Most of the time, it was wide enough that the average kid could jump across it in most places or wade through it with no trouble. It was behind our house, streaming through the bottom of a bank about three-feet deep. We used to play in the creek as there were always small fish, frogs, snakes, turtles, spiders, and all sorts of fun little-boy things living there. One day, somebody suggested we build a dam and watch to see what would happen. After all, we knew about beavers and had seen their dams in the river, which wasn't too far away. Somehow, someone came up with the idea of using burlap bags. One of things little boys intuitively know is that burlap bags filled with dirt would make a nifty dam. And so, we went to work filling burlap bags in hopes of equaling the expertise of the beavers. I have no memory of where the burlap bags came from, but we sure had a bunch of them; somebody probably stole them from around the mill. Or maybe I found them around Dad's Store.

Needless to say, nobody could have paid us enough money to do this much work if it was required of us, but away we worked tirelessly until we had a dam about two-feet high. Think back to what I said earlier about Tom Sawyer and the opening scene of him white washing the fence. That was us. Three or four little boys who ordinarily would run from any kind of physical labor. But here we are gathering up shovels and burlap bags at the edge of this creek on what was probably a reasonably warm summer's day. It was seldom hot in Canton, as I later learned when I lived in places where it got hot in the summer. I believe we started digging the sandy wet dirt out of the bottom of the creek itself but soon figured out that wet dirt would be too heavy to deal with. The next best place was to just dig out the sides of the bank, so we filled the 6 or 10 bags we eventually used—I have no real recollection of exactly how many bags we filled— with the soft loamy dirt, weeds and all from the bank. It must not have been particularly hard work and playing in dirt was always fun, because we did complete the task and were able to pile the bags, one on top of the other.

We stacked the bags like you would a brick wall, alternating them to give our wall maximum strength and we saw immediate results of our work. I think we realized within a few short minutes that we may have not thought this through quite far enough. By the time we were done, the water was already backing up and there was nothing we could do about it because we quickly realized that we couldn't easily undo what we had created as the bags got very heavy as soon as they got wet. Our engineering skills did not go so far as to consider adding an overflow pipe or drain in the middle; after all, I doubt that it occurred to us that this contraption might actually work. Uh oh.

Well, it worked. In fact, our dam was better than any beavers had ever built on that creek. A day or two later, we went down to look at our handiwork and discovered that the water was backing up behind the dam and the creek bed was drying up in front of the dam—uh, oh. We looked at each other, bursting simultaneously with pride and fear wondering, "What now?" After deciding that the water backing up wasn't a good situation, and since we had no plans for what to do to rectify the problem, we did what any red-blooded boys would do. We hid, pretending not to notice and told no one.

We watched in horror and curiosity as the water continued to back up. The yards of homeowners far upstream soon started flooding. Downstream, gardeners who depended on the creek to water their gardens wondered what happened to the creek. The water level behind our house started to reach our own yard. Big trouble loomed. Doomsday was about to arrive.

Homeowners up and down the creek started walking the bank to see where the problem was and soon, our doorbell was ringing. "Who the hell!" "What idiot built that dam?!" "Joseph, get in here, NOW!" "Who, me?" Oh, how I related to Tom Sawyer! My father was not happy.

You might think that part of a just punishment would be to destroy the dam. Unfortunately, it was too well-built to simply take down what we put up. As we learned, sand is the traditional material for this because it allows for very slow pour-through of water over time, but dirt is more dense—especially the dirt in that part of the country. It soaked up water for days, and the sunshine served as a nice oven making something very close to concrete; completely immovable by human hands.

There was no way a couple of little boys were going to destroy that dam. It took men with picks and shovels and a lot of sweat to finally break it apart and get the water flowing again. Destroying this thing turned out to be a serious problem and Dad got a lot of grief for it. The burlap bags had pretty much disintegrated and the weeds that had been picked up with dirt thrived in the flowing water, so it was much more than just a pile of dirt in the middle of the creek. I don't remember how many men worked on it to take it apart or how long it took, but it wasn't a simple task and we stayed out of the way so I didn't see exactly what they did or how they did it. But given its location, it all had to be done by hand because in those days there weren't the kind of small front loaders that could be brought in today.

Johnson Drive is about a quarter-mile or so long and the creek flows behind everyone's house, so every back yard was flooded. Two or three houses past ours, the back yards are about level with the creek bed so the water came well up into the yards and probably ruined gardens, flowers, and who knows what else. Downstream, of course, there was no water and the people depended on the creek to water some fairly large gardens. In terms of little boy escapades this one ranks pretty high on the all time list. Eventually it was cleared and the water flowed again in its normal course. We were strictly forbidden from going near the creek or playing in it or ever again attempting to build a dam. What other punishments we suffered, I have no memory.

Boy Scouts

As a Boy Scout, I went to Boy Scout camp and went on overnight hiking trips. That was fun and in many ways it prepared me for the Army because I learned many survival skills and knew I could get along in some tough situations. Camp Daniel Boone is still operating in Haywood County although I haven't been back to see it.

Let's go back to my buddies, the guys in the Boy Scouts. These were guys who lived primarily on Johnson Street and the area still known as Highland Park. About ten of us ran around together pretty regularly from about second grade until I left town after tenth grade. We got into some pretty interesting trouble over the years and had a lot fun together.

One memorable July 4th night we ended up seeing the inside of the town jail briefly for making a public nuisance, getting caught with firecrackers, and generally being stupid. One of our gang was the son of the mayor, and all of our fathers had to come down and retrieve us. There were no other repercussions, other than being scared to death. It was the only time in my life I actually saw the inside of a jail cell, and it was frightening, even with the door left open. I suppose I should tell you what we were doing to end up going to jail. Looking back, today's kids would think it wasn't a big deal. My how times have changed. First of all, firecrackers and all fireworks were illegal in North Carolina so just possessing them was the first infraction, and a big deal, but everyone had a least a few. Canton is only 30 or 40 miles from the South Carolina state line where fireworks are perfectly legal—need I say more? On every festive occasion, those with cars gathered up money from those in need of fireworks and took off for the nearest border crossing, coming back with a trunk full of firecrackers, cherry bombs, sparklers, and rockets of various kinds. Then there were those wonderful little tiny balls that you throw down the hall in school and when stepped on would explode under unsuspecting feet of, hopefully, GIRLS.

So here we were on July 4th with our illegal supply of firecrackers stuffed in our pockets out looking for trouble, wandering around the neighborhood. At the top of the hill were some empty trash cans. In those days trash cans were large and heavy, made of metal; none of that flimsy plastic stuff, which hadn't been invented yet. "Say," we thought, "Wouldn't it be fun to fill those trash cans with some firecrackers and set them off rolling down this hill?" Wow, what a terrific idea! And so we did. Two or three big metal trash cans went rolling down a hill with firecrackers exploding making just the kind of obnoxious racket we hoped for, but at just the wrong moment. The trash cans rolled down the hill just as this nice police car comes rolling up the hill! How's that for timing? And away we go, as fast as we can run, which wasn't fast enough to outrun the law, and soon enough we're in the back seat of a police car on our way to the police station and into a jail cell. We spent the rest of our July 4th with very unhappy fathers, but it was worth every minute, looking back.

We went on hikes and camping trips in the summer up in the mountains and once completed a five-day hike. The Appalachian Trail wasn't always open like it is now and there was a time in the mid-1950s when an effort was made to reopen it. I believe they assigned chunks of it to various Boy Scout troops, and our troop was assigned a piece from somewhere near Canton to the Tennessee border. We went up there and spent five days hacking underbrush with machetes. Now there's an image that might be hard for people today to believe—a dozen or so young teenage boys swinging sharp machetes and running loose in the woods. But no one got hurt as we spent our time clearing a piece of the trail. I don't know how long our section was, it might have been a few miles. I remember we ended up in Tennessee where we were picked up by our parents and driven home, exhausted, but having had the experience of our young lives.

My most memorable story of that time in life was getting bitten by a rattlesnake. I was saved by the fact that I had on tall, heavy, leather boots that came up my calf, and they were loose on me because my legs were rather skinny. The snake's teeth punctured the leather and missed my ankle or my calf by a fraction of an inch. He dug his fangs right through the leather and held on thinking that he had me. The scouts were yelling, "Don't move! Don't move!" The scoutmaster quickly grabbed a hatchet, cut down a small sapling with one motion and beat the snake over the head with it and killed it. It was a pretty good-sized snake, probably three or four feet long. We cut off his head and his tail. I kept his tail as a souvenir, because it contained the rattles, then we skinned him and cooked the meat for dinner by wrapping it around a stick and cooking it over an open fire. The rattlesnake missed out on his adventure, but we sure didn't. I don't have a good memory of what it tasted like, probably like chicken, which is what everyone says things taste like when you've never eaten it before. Everything cooked over an open fire like that has that wonderfully memorable smoky flavor anyway.

We stretched out the skin to dry and I took it home for my mother. When I showed her the rattlesnake skin and the rattles and told her the story, she was very excited as you might imagine. If you have a Jewish mother, I'm sure you understand how pleased she was to know that her son had gotten bitten by a rattlesnake and he was home, telling the story of his exploit, and presenting her with this trophy. That's always been one of my favorite stories. I kept the rattles for quite a while, but they eventually disappeared. It was a fun trip and was the longest camping trip we ever took. I went back up there with the scouts a couple more times to do work on the Appalachian Trail, but we usually stayed only for one or two nights.

One of my other favorite stories of being up in the mountains was the time we ran into some moonshiners. We were walking along a ridge and these two guys came up on us from below. They looked like something out of the eighteenth or nineteenth century. They were wearing dirty coveralls and they had long, scraggly beards. One of them said something like, "Where y'all goin?" And the scoutmaster said, "We're just Boy Scouts walking along the ridge. We're go'n up yonder."

The fellows stared back at us and the one said, "Well now, y'all don't be goin' down off'n this here ridge. What's down thar, why that's none y'all's businesses. Don't y'all be goin' down thar."

Of course we had an idea what was going on down thar, and we had no intention of investigating. They were carrying ancient muzzle-loading rifles. Nobody believes that, but it's true. These were old-time moonshiners whose families and their ancestors had been up in those hills forever.

I was in the scouts for a number of years and went to Boy Scout camp two or three summers to a campground called Camp Daniel Boone that is still up there, out past Canton. I advanced as far as Life Scout, which is the rank just below Eagle. I didn't make it to the top rank because of issues that I felt were caused by some anti-Semitism. That was the only time that

I felt that my being Jewish was an issue in Western North Carolina as I was growing up in Canton. It's something that happened, and I will not mention it again.

All in all, I think that growing up in Canton was idyllic. I certainly had no idea what was going on in the rest of the world.

We didn't have television until sometime in the mid-1950s, and then I think we only had one channel. The first newscast we saw was the Huntley-Brinkley Report as I recall. I can remember watching news reports of the Korean War, and when the war started to come to an end I wondered what they could possibly report about when there was no more war. What will there be to talk about? The things that go through children's minds.

Joe & Morty, Academy St. Canton, NC 1948

Dad, Uncle Max, Grandma Kaplan & Uncle Bernie
(Front) Judy, Morty & Alan
Pisgah Dr., Canton 1953

Family history

All my life, people have asked me what was it like to grow up Jewish as the only Jews in a small town in the South. But of course, that being my only experience of growing up, I never thought about it until people started asking me. Now I think about it a lot and about what growing up means. I think about the years that went by and how they seemed at the time, while we were living them. I suppose it's a cliché or axiomatic to say that as we look back from adulthood, or as in my case when I feel I'm entering old age, to say that the years compress. To a ten-year-old child, are ten years a lifetime? Today, ten years isn't a very long time. We actually only lived in that small town, Canton, from 1946 to 1957, and then moved to Asheville either at the end of 1957 or early 1958. So, I lived in Canton from the time I was about 3 and a half until I was about 15, I suppose those were the years we refer to as growing up.

Before going on, I want to give you a brief history of my family and how we got to Canton.

I was born on October 17, 1942, in Waterbury, Connecticut. What my parents were doing in Waterbury, Connecticut raises a number of stories, and I cannot even get past that date without having to tell some of them. First, I already had a big brother; Mort was born in Scranton, PA on May 17, 1940. The war was on when both of us were born, but, of course, we didn't know that. And we didn't know that it was to be a part of our lives for all of our lives. I cannot know why my parents went from Scranton to

Waterbury, that's lost to history; I don't know what the world was like that caused or forced them to move. So, before we can move past my own birth, I have to go back and talk about the stories that I've heard all of my life about what was going on between their times in Scranton and Waterbury.

As I heard it, Dad needed to find a job and heard there was factory work in Connecticut, and he ended up working in a war factory making nose cones for some kind of bombs. He brought some of them home and we played with them for years after the war until they got lost, or eventually, Mom threw them out. The problem with that story is that there are also stories about how Dad and his brothers and parents had a farm in Montrose, PA, where they also hauled timber and coal. So why did Dad all of sudden have to pick up and move and take a factory job? Maybe there was fighting in the family.

Much later, after the Korean war, Dad's brothers Bernie and Seymour were building homes together in suburban Philadelphia, and I witnessed some knock-down, drag-out fights, so I know that there were some serious tempers in my family. (Of course, present company is excepted from the Kaplan temper!) Mom didn't like fighting, and the story was that she was afraid of her father-in-law, and she and uncle Bernie didn't get along so great. I vaguely remember hearing that either Grampa or Grandma looked down on her and treated her like a servant so maybe that contributed to why they moved away.

If you knew my dad, you would know he was not a guy to stand in a factory for eight hours a day making nose cones for a bomb or doing any kind of repetitive work. So that job didn't last very long. Apparently Mom was pregnant when they moved to Waterbury, and the job lasted about long enough for me to be born, and then it was back to Scranton, or possibly Binghamton, NY, for some period and then to Scranton. For some reason known only to fate, a book of World War II ration stamps has survived all these years, and I still have it in my possession. There are some in my name, some in Mort's, some in Mom's. They show an address in Binghamton, NY so we obviously lived there for a while. I don't remember much about any of that, of course. I know we were living in Scranton when Dad got back from Japan because that is where we were when Uncle Seymour painted the famous portrait—famous in our family, anyway which is the front cover of this book—of me and Morty sitting on a footstool waiting for Daddy to come home. It is signed and dated 1945, Scranton, PA.

Now which way should I go with this story? Should I go forward with my life or should I go backward and talk about my parents' lives? I think I'll back up for some of the history of my parents' lives and then go forward with my life and maybe include some other stories later about my parents to fill in some of the gaps.

My parents were Molly and Louis Kaplan. Dad was born in Greenport, Long Island, NY. Greenport is so far east on Long Island that if you try to keep going east the next land is England. Dad's grandparents, Isaac and Bryna Kaplan, immigrated from Russia about 1870 bringing with them two sons, one of which was Dads' father, Hyman. Information on the other son has been lost. They are believed to have come from the Ukraine, most probably from an area near the city of Odessa or the Black Sea area, exactly where is lost to history. As so many of the Russian Jewish immigrants who started coming here then and for the next 50 or 60 years, I think we can assume he was leaving to get away from the Army draft (which was typically 25 years), the general poverty of the times, and the pogroms that made life miserable for the Jews under the rule of the Czar.

Pogrom is a Russian word designating an attack, accompanied by destruction, looting of property, murder, and rape, perpetrated by one section of the population against another. In modern Russian history pogroms have been perpetrated against other nations (Armenians, Tatars) or groups of inhabitants (intelligentsia). However, as an international term, the word pogrom is employed in many languages to describe specifically the attacks accompanied by looting and bloodshed against the Jews in Russia. The pogroms of the 1880s took place during the period of confusion which prevailed in Russia after the assassination of Czar Alexander II by members of the revolutionary organization Narodnaya Volya on March 13, 1881. Anti-Jewish circles spread a rumor that the czar had been assassinated by Jews and that the government had authorized attacks on them.

How did he end up in Greenport? What was Greenport? I have never been there and have never met any of my cousins but have always known that there was and is a substantial extended family of descendants of Isaac and Bryna. My grandfather, Hyman, was one of five brothers and two sisters. Lots of Kaplans. One of the brothers was at some point thrown out of the family for some infraction of the religious rules of the time. It was told to me that he violated the observance of the High Holy Days and was ostracized for his behavior. He left Greenport, and the last that was ever known of him was that he ended somewhere in Oklahoma in the oil *bidness*, married a Christian woman, converted, changed his name, and disappeared from the family.

In doing my research for this book I made contact with some of these cousins and found one in New York who has been keeping a completed family tree of all of the descendants of Isaac and Bryna. I helped him bring it up to date with the last couple of generations of our branch and we hope to meet in the near future.

By the late 19th century the eastern end of Long Island was a farming and fishing economy and Greenport as a thriving deep-water port. For ships sailing north from New York to Boston, Greenport was the next deep water port where they could pull in to load and unload, buy and sell, pick up and drop off passengers. Isaac arrived in New York. Did he know anyone? In my reading about 19th and early 20th century immigration, I found a cliché, a joke, that said that every young Jew who landed in New York had an uncle who was already here and he had his uncle's name sewn somewhere in his clothes. Did Isaac have an Uncle already here? Or, in this case was Isaac the first of our line of Kaplans? We don't know, and here we are four or five generations removed with no way to find out. Somehow Isaac got on a ship going north. Did he really want to go to Boston? There were recruiters from many cities up and down the coast, from Charleston and Richmond in the South and Boston in the North, looking for young men for all kinds of labor: to work in the fields, in shops, to peddle merchandise, etc. Perhaps he was recruited, who knows.

The family story is that Isaac had two unique and salable skills. First of all, he knew multiple languages: probably Russian, Hebrew, Yiddish, Polish, Ukrainian, and various local dialects. Secondly he was a horseman. Apparently he had worked on and perhaps been a manager of the estate of one of the larger landowning princes in the areas he lived in and learned to manage horses. Not only to manage horses but to understand horses and was skilled in buying and selling horses. However it worked out he went to Greenport where he found employment on the farms out there to do the two things that fit his skills. Because of his language skills he was able to go back to the New York and recruit labor and bring men (and I assume women and families) back to work the farms and fields. And because horses were a primary need for work and transportation he would buy and sell horses for the farms and the town as well. He apparently prospered and raised a family in his new home and new country. My great grandfather Isaac.

By the early 20th century, there was a thriving Jewish community in Greenport; I have a booklet that was put together sometime in the 1980s that is compilation of board minutes from the founding of the synagogue, Congregation Tifereth Israel Anshei Greenport, that mentions the marriage of my grandparents, Hyman and Hannah and the birth of my father, Louis.

Later, it also mentions how as a young adult, Hyman was thrown out for misbehaving and fighting over some issue or other. This is not surprising—remember what I said about the Kaplan temper and fighting. I have never visited Greenport, but it has always been on my list of things to do. There is still a Zelig Kaplan in Greenport, a cousin I recently contacted who is only a few weeks older than me and the grandson of one of my grandfather's brothers. We had a long talk and he filled me in on some of these details. There are whole families of cousins I've never met scattered around New York City and state. It is a long drive, but maybe I still will visit and meet them someday. One other little sidebar: I have a son, Jeffrey. My cousin David has a son Jeffrey almost exactly the same age and Zelig told me that another cousin has a Jeffrey about the same age. What is with this genetic thing, anyway?

I don't know the story of how Dad's father ended up marrying my grandmother and how they then all ended up in Scranton. Around 1900, my grandmother, Hannah Minsky, came to the United States from the Belarus region, from a small town somewhere in the area of Minsk. Her story of walking across Europe to Bremerhaven would fill another book if I could only remember all of her adventures. She was just 15 or 16 years old when she emigrated through Ellis Island along with the other millions of Russians and other Eastern Europeans who came in the 50 or so years from about 1880 to about 1927 when the American government closed the door to immigration, a bad decision that we see the results of to this day. A visit to the Lower East Side, to Ellis Island (now a museum), and to the Tenement Museum are a must for anyone who wishes to understand how all of those millions of people were brought into this country and how they lived and how they survived.

She lived and worked in the famous Lower East Side of Manhattan where so many Jews settled at that time. One job she had was pushing one of the push carts that you may have heard or read about. For a person who got off the boat with no money, no English, no skills except the willingness to work, there weren't many ways to start earning a living, and the way many people started out was by peddling merchandise on the street. At the very bottom were those who carried a pack on their back and sold whatever they could carry, then went back to whatever merchant they were working for and bought more merchandise, and went back out in the street or door to door with another load. At some point they would work themselves up to be able to afford a two-wheeled cart that could be loaded with merchandise and pushed up and down the street or eventually, perhaps, parked in a more or less permanent spot. These were called push carts. I suppose the next level would to be able to afford a larger cart and a horse and be able to carry more merchandise and travel further. Many large fortunes were eventually made this way, many people eventually opened department stores and became famous names that we know today. As I said earlier, Jews who got off the boat at Ellis Island had an uncle who was already here who he could go to for a small loan to help him or her get started with a load of merchandise or a job in his store or factory and that is the way they all got started.

I don't know what my Grandmother was like as a young woman, but she was a tough, loving, wonderful Grandma whom I knew rather well as I grew up.

Dad was the oldest of four sons who grew up in Scranton: Morris, Bernie, and Seymour were his brothers. Among the unknown stories is the migration from Greenport to Scranton. We don't know why they left. But, Dad met Mom in Scranton; they married and eventually had four children.

Mom also was the daughter of Eastern European immigrants. Her father was said to have been from Austria, but it may just as well have been Poland or Lithuania as the borders of the countries—and the countries themselves—are not what we know them to be today and her mother is believed to have been from the same area, although they met here, not in Europe.

From the stories she told us, I believe she grew up in extreme poverty as one of seven children. Her father had a small grocery store; it might have been a candy store, the story kept changing. Her father was extremely religious and only worked enough to put the bare minimum of food on the table so that he could have enough time for prayers and study.

Mom's mother was from Austria/Hungary and had a daughter of indeterminate fatherhood prior to marrying Mom's father; Mom's father had two sons who were born back in what was said to be Austria, but the borders of those countries changed so much at the end of the 19th century that one never knew exactly where the boundaries of those countries were. Her father had already emigrated, but his first wife died before he could bring her over with the boys, David and Henry, who essentially were left as orphans in the small shtetl as the Jewish villages were known in that era. The townspeople couldn't afford to feed them, so they were sent on their own to find their way to America. They had to walk, first to Bremerhaven or Hanover, the two German cities from which ships took emigrants to America. They were very young, either 9 and 11 or 11 and 13, and they were all alone. It took them two years to walk across Europe, and they suffered terrible hardships, but eventually they made it to New York and somehow, they found their father. That story was told to me by my cousin, Sally, who is Henry's daughter. Mom's mother and father, Isaac and Anna Pollack, had four more children together: Max, Lou, Molly (Mom), and Sam, all born in Scranton, PA. One interesting little sidebar that we always like to joke about is that Mom's brother, Lou, married a girl named Molly and Lou and Molly had a daughter Judy. My mother, Molly, married a man named Lou, and Molly and Lou also had a daughter named Judy. That's a brief history of Mom and Dad.

Back to my story

Getting back to my story: As I said, I was born in Waterbury, CT. We lived there for a short time and went back to Scranton sometime in 1943. World War II was on, and Dad got drafted at some point, and he went off to the Pacific Theater. Mom had two children to take care of, but she had her whole family and Dad's family all living in and around Scranton, so she had help.

Our family history at this point includes **THE FARM**, which I put in bold capital letters because it was a folly of my grandfather's that ultimately caused a great deal of family strife. At some time in the 1930s my grandfather Kaplan decided that buying a farm near Montrose, PA, would be a good idea. I can only conjecture that he must have thought it was a good way to survive the Depression and perhaps foresaw the coming war in Europe. In any case I have no actual memory of the farm, only all the stories I heard of it and the pictures you see in this book. I probably was there as a baby and Morty says he remembers being there. Eventually it was sold when Dad was away in the Army in the Pacific and the proceeds were divided up; but I always had the feeling that it was not done fairly and Dad and Mom felt that they didn't get what they were entitled to. That may have been one of the incentives for leaving for North Carolina.

In 1943 we're in Scranton. That is me, Morty, and Mom, plus the whole extended family. At some point Dad is drafted into the Army then was home because Judy was born in May of 1945 and then Dad is somewhere in the South Pacific. Various uncles are fighting the war in other parts of the world. But our lives quickly change, because by sometime in late 1946, we're in Canton, NC, and in March 1947, there are four children instead of two.

A lot happened: Dad was fighting with the Army on the island of Luzon in the Philippines, preparing to invade Japan when the bomb was dropped on Hiroshima and Nagasaki, and thank God it was, because it brought about the end of the war. From there, Dad was with the occupation forces in Tokyo for a while. I never did quite understand the timing of when he was in Japan or how long he was there. He told stories of being with families, and I remember him telling of having dinner and being very welcomed by the Japanese families that he met. He brought home souvenirs, souvenir dishes and chopsticks, and he brought Mom a Japanese flag that she wore as a scarf. But I don't know exactly how long he was there. I do know that he was afraid to fly home and instead he took a boat. I have no idea how long that must've taken. While he was on his way home on the boat, Uncle Seymour painted the famous portrait of me and Morty that now hangs in my house and is the cover of this book. It was a gift for Dad.

Grandma Kaplan on the tractor sans hat and gloves in the snow
Montrose, PA, December 1942

Being Jewish in Canton

I've written the stories of how we got to Canton, but why did we come to Canton of all places? I've been asked what it was like being Jewish in such a small town. Were there other Jews in other small towns around the mountains? Who were they; how did they get there? That led me to start thinking about the history of the Jews in Western North Carolina.

The earliest Jewish settler I can find in Henderson County is Captain John Levi who came to Henderson County from Charleston, South Carolina in about 1830 when he landed with the British Navy as a Drum Major. At that time Charleston was the largest, busiest port on the Eastern seaboard of the United States. In 1834 he married Sarah Bailey. In 1835 he accompanied General Samuel, "Sam," Houston fighting in the War of Independence as part of the winning effort to bring Texas into the United States as a constituent state. John was given a Texas land grant that he sold when he and Sarah moved to the Bob's Creek area in Zirconia, NC. There, he built a farm on top of Panther Mountain. He had five sons who all joined the Confederacy of the United States, more commonly referred to simply as the Confederacy, and one daughter. John Levi's descendants in Henderson County have fought in every war involving the U.S. He is buried in the Fruitland Cemetery in Henderson County. There doesn't seem to be any historical connection to the Levi family and any later Jewish migration to the area, and it can be assumed that the Levis intermarried into the neighboring Christian community. There are a number of Levi families throughout the area who are not Jewish.

Jews apparently began a slow migration into the mountains later in the 19th century and at an increasing pace in the early 20th century, especially into Asheville and Hendersonville. By the 1890s, they were forming synagogues in Asheville and, in 1922, formed the only synagogue in Hendersonville, Agudas Israel Congregation, which still exists today.

Jewish families migrated out to even more remote towns to the north and west of Asheville, although not in large enough numbers to sustain a synagogue or Jewish Community Center. When we lived in Canton, we were friends with families or at least knew other Jews in Brevard, Waynesville, and Sylva where we were friends with the Shulmans, Lessings, and Karps (all three of whom owned clothing stores in that small town, Murphy, where Sam Kaye lived and who helped Dad open his store). These families had arrived well before us in 1946, some by a generation or more. They were almost all merchants of one kind or another. Many had started out as peddlers traveling by horseback or pulling a wagon, buying and selling a variety of goods until they finally settled down. Why they chose these backwoods, out-of-the-way places is a mystery we'll never answer. Perhaps it resembled the small towns they came from in Eastern Europe.

In his book, Down Home, Jewish Life in North Carolina, Leonard Rogoff, explores in great depth the history of the migration of the Jews, primarily from Eastern Europe, through New York and down the coast to North Carolina. He tells stories of how immigrants arrived penniless with only their ambition and willingness to work hard, how they became peddlers sometimes carrying goods on their backs and working their way to a horse and wagon to opening a store. Through success and failure some became incredibly wealthy and those who succeeded almost invariably helped those who came behind them. Remember the joke that every Jew who got off the boat in New York had an uncle who was already here who you could look up and he'd lend him a hand to get started if he was willing to work.

In his book, Rogoff tells the story of the Epstein family of Baltimore, Maryland and the Baltimore Bargain House. Throughout the South, every small town had one or more Jewish-owned clothing store. In many cases that store owner got his start by going to the Baltimore Bargain House where he could get merchandise on credit to stock his shelves, pay for his inventory when he was able at the end of the season, and then go back for more. As long as he kept current they would advance him inventory on credit. In that way, the Epsteins became incredibly prosperous and towns throughout the South had many Jewish clothing merchants.

The book is full of tales of how the Jews of North Carolina lived and prospered and failed and suffered and built communities and synagogues. Anyone interested in personal histories should take a look at this very readable book.

Some of these families made an effort to retain their religion and pass it on to their children—my contemporaries—and some didn't. Some of my friends from those families intermarried and converted to Christianity and stayed in the towns they grew up in. Others got out, went on to college, and became very successful in a variety of fields and endeavors. Occasionally, over the years, a name will pop up in the news or on a book cover or there will be a reunion and someone we know will have become famous, and we will marvel at who came out of the backwoods of Western North Carolina.

Now, we were part of this ongoing migration of Jews into the mountains looking for a new life. One thing was for certain, my parents were very Jewish. They came from religious, orthodox backgrounds. Dad studied to be a rabbi, and they intended to keep a religious, kosher home. So, why would they come to live in a place with no other Jews, no Jewish life for their children and then make demands on their children that they identify as being Jews? I don't have the answers and it remains the central question and mystery of my life. I don't think any of us, Morty, Judy or Alan, ever actually asked them that question directly.

I had a bunch of guys I ran around with in Canton. I matured rather late, so I didn't pay a lot of attention to girls until I got to Asheville. There was a major problem having to do with girls in Canton. You see, because we were Jewish, Mom and Dad brought us up to believe that we could only go out with Jewish girls. You see the irony in this, right? What the hell are we doing in a town like Canton? After all, we're now four kids, but we can only go out with Jewish girls, or boys in Judy's case, and we're growing up in a town with no other Jews. Mom and Dad's answer was that there are Jews in Asheville, and we belong to the synagogue and the Jew- ish community center there, so we will meet other Jewish children in Asheville.

Well, that didn't really work because we spent our days with the children from school in Canton. I think Morty went out with some girls in Canton in spite of the rules; I guess it didn't hurt him because he went on to become a rabbi. I didn't date because I wasn't particularly interested in girls until I was well into high school, and by that time we had moved to Asheville. So, for me it wasn't much of a problem, but it was a strange situation.

Even in Asheville, however, it was troublesome because there were only a few Jewish girls of the appropriate age to date and even fewer of them were interested in going out with me. Whether any of the non-Jewish girls would have been interested, I never explored. In those days girls didn't call boys, at least none were calling me. Aside from everything else I was too naïve and unaware to have recognized any girl expressing an interest in me short of being hit over the head.

Other *being Jewish* issues

Dad was very much involved in the local community. I don't think it had anything to do with his business, as he wasn't the kind of person to look at civic affairs as a way to build his business, although they obviously went together. I recall him going to Lion's Club meetings and to Toastmasters International, the two that he seemed to be the most involved in. The Lions were then, and I believe still are involved in issues related to raising money to help the blind. I have no idea what he actually did, but I know he went to meetings and was active. Toastmasters was about learning to give speeches and I remember him writing and practicing his speeches. I think he must have been very good at public speaking because he was an intelligent, well-educated man who read a great deal and could talk about most things to just about anyone who wanted to listen. My guess is he talked mostly about history, religion, and Judaism, but I could be wrong. It would be nice to know.

In addition to civic organizations, Dad got involved in local politics and I believe was, at one time, on the town council and served as chairman of the Civil Defense Corps, a civilian organization whose mission it was to educate the public and protect the Unites States from the dangers of atomic attack during the early Cold War era. It is important to understand what a big deal that was in the 1950s. This was the era when the Atomic Bomb threat from Communist Soviet Union/Russia was the real deal. The incredible and frightening casualties resulting from the U.S. attacks on Hiroshima and Nagasaki, Japan, was still fresh news. Everyone knew what a danger an atomic bomb was; that we had them and the Russians had stolen our secrets and now they had them and were threatening us and our way of life. So, every city and town in America had a Civil Defense Corps of some kind and had to develop a plan to protect its citizens. Dad was in charge in Canton. What did the plan amount to? All I remember were the

Duck and Cover drills where we all had to hide under our desks in schools until the air defense sirens stopped blasting and we could get up and go back to our lessons. Somehow, nuclear radiation couldn't or wouldn't dare penetrate the hard wood of those specially made hundred-year-old desks. They sure managed to scare us to death, or at least our mothers, I suppose. The general feeling was that, "No damn fool Russkies would come to these-here parts and challenges us mountain folks up here in these here hills and hollers! No siree-Bob. We'd give'm what fer!" Or some such talk. I've included this discussion under the Jewish issues subheading to try to show that I don't remember a lot of actual Jewish issues growing up in Canton.

One of Dad's other community activities he both delighted in and was always frustrated by was his relationship with the local churches and ministers. My view is that he must have felt that the best way to defuse any potential anti-Semitic problems was through a proactive attempt at education. To that end, he was always attempting to have friendly relations with any and all of the local church leaders and ministers who would talk with him, debate, discuss, study, and invite him to their churches to teach their congregations about Judaism and Jewish issues. Over the years, he and our family, became quite friendly with a few of these men and women, and their families, and I believe he had some success. Dad, as I have said, was an intellectual who loved a good intellectual discussion, so having stuck himself away in this backwater town, he didn't find a lot of people to talk to, but he did find a couple of these ministers with whom he could have a good relationship.

And so, he was invited to teach Sunday school at various churches, and he even was invited to either teach or give guest lectures at some of the smaller religious-oriented colleges around Western North Carolina. But, there was an inevitable problem that he almost always came home complaining about. It seems that no matter what the subject, always some aspect of the Bible probably relating to some imminent holiday, no matter how hard he tried to get across the uniquely Jewish perspective, someone (often including the minister of the church) would want to know where his/our belief in Jesus fit in. Now, he had no problem with the Christian beliefs, he just wanted to get across the ideas that there could be other beliefs without Jesus, but it was not to be—ever. He was never interested in converting anyone, just trying to express a different concept, and he never gave up. I should add here that Uncle Morris in Hendersonville was active in much the same way, and they would often share their experiences with the local churches and express the same frustrations with trying to get their points across. Both Dad and Uncle Morris were very influential in their respective towns in fostering good interfaith relations.

Another facet of our religious life intersecting with our Christian neighbors was the various holidays we celebrated and our attempts to share those holidays with our friends and neighbors. My favorite holiday was and has always been Passover (Pesach). I am hardly unique in the view that Passover is the most widely observed Jewish holiday of all the Jewish Holidays around the world. Jews who seldom acknowledge any other facet or aspect of their being Jewish will in some way acknowledge Passover with some form of a Seder, the traditional meal which encompasses telling the story of the Exodus from Egypt 3,500 years ago, the seminal story of the Jewish people.

In our house, the Passover Seder was always a grand event, a tradition that I kept in my own home. I can never remember a Seder with fewer than 18 or 20 people, sometimes 25 or more. Kids, parents, grandparents, pandemonium, food, wine, fights, and running around the table. Adults trying to say the traditional prayers and the story while the kids are whining about when dinner is going to be served. What fun! The point of the Passover Seder is to tell the story of the Exodus from Egypt, the redemption of the Jews, Moses and Mount Sinai, and most important, to pass the tradition from one generation to the next. Having multiple generations at the table so the children can hear the stories of the parents and the grandparents, and maybe an old great-grandparent, talk about what their Seder was like is how that is accomplished. To share that experience with friends from the community is to show who we are and what Judaism is about. Today, I meet people who still remember my parents because 50 or 60 years ago, they were at a Seder at our house in Canton or Asheville.

Hot dog

One birthday, my 10th or 11th maybe, my mother decided I would have a party in the back yard and should invite all my friends; we would have a cookout and grill hot dogs. Uh, kosher hot dogs, mind you, that's the point of this particular story. Remember where we are.

The house in Canton on Pisgah Drive had a nice back yard with a little creek in the back; the one with bamboo growing—where we built the dam that caused so much trouble— and over the side by the road we tried growing a garden for a couple of summers. No green thumbs in this gang, however. At the other end of the yard Dad built a fireplace out of bricks. Either they didn't sell barbecue grills you could buy at Sears yet, or he wasn't about to buy anything for more money that wouldn't work as well when he could build it.

Here we were a bunch of 10- or 11-year-olds in the back yard doing what little boys do at a birthday party, running around, making noise, playing football, eating hot dogs, potato salad, birthday cake, and whatever else, generally having a good time. I only vaguely remember the whole affair. I have no idea what I got for that birthday that year. What I do remember vividly was that there weren't enough hot dogs. Everybody loved the hot dogs. Did I say they were Hebrew National from Schandler's Deli in Asheville? How many of those kids do you think ever had been to

Schandler's? Or knew what a kosher hot dog was? Or Hebrew National? Uh Oh! By the way, you had to have lived in Asheville a long time ago to have bought a hot dog from Aaron Schandler, may he rest in peace. A nice man who gave me my first taste of kosher salami, real swiss cheese with holes in it, and other traditional Jewish deli food. Every Sunday we went there to stock up on the things that the grocery stores didn't sell, and my mother invariable complained about the prices.

Well, all my little friends went home and told their moms about the party and about the hot dogs, and the phone started to ring. The moms wanted to know about the hot dogs, what were they, and what were we feeding their kids? And where did you get them? And then, a big ooops, what did they cost? You spent *how much* for a hot dog!? Uh oh! Mom was in big trouble. Needless to say, there were no more cookout birthday parties at the Kaplan's.

Flash ahead

I attended my Canton High School graduating class's 50th reunion in June of 2010. I didn't actually graduate with that class as we had moved to Asheville and I finished high school at Lee H. Edwards—since renamed Asheville High School.

Rewind some five years earlier, to the spring of 2005. My cell phone rang one Saturday evening as we were about to start dinner at a friend's house in Tampa, Florida, where we were living at the time. Much to my surprise, it was a voice I hadn't heard since probably 1957 or '58, my old friend Ricky Briggs. Ricky and I and been friends since kindergarten. He had an older brother, Bruce, who was Morty's friend, and our parents were friends with his mother, so he was truly a long-lost friend and someone I was pleased to hear from. Ricky has a distinctive voice that retains the old mountain accent that is easy to recognize, even after all these years.

It was about seven o'clock Saturday night and our friends had just put dinner on the table. I answered my phone and, with a glimmer of recognition, I answered, "Yes" when Ricky asked, "Is this Joseph Kaplan?"

"The Joseph Kaplan of the Canton, North Carolina, Kaplans?"

"Yes," I said, amazed and surprised. "Who is this? Ricky?"

Ricky said, "Why, yes. This is Ricky Briggs from Canton and we've been looking for you for the last 45 years. Where have you been?"

He always called me Joseph. Ricky was always very formal that way. Still is.

We talked for a few minutes and I told him where I was, that I would call him back after dinner, and we hung up. In some ways, that phone call launched this whole process of reconnecting with my past, with Canton, with the way I grew up, with telling all these stories, with wanting to write them down, with thinking maybe there was something worth preserving in the way life was in that place at that time.

When I called back, Ricky told me that the Canton High graduation class of 1960 was planning their 45th reunion. I reminded him that I had left after the 10th grade and he told me it didn't matter, that they were trying to find as many people as they could who had been kids in Canton from the late '40s through the early '60s whether or not they graduated in 1960. They had been looking for me and Morty for years and his brother, Bruce, had heard from a friend that Morty had become a rabbi. They contacted him and got my number. As a result, my wife, Sue, and I were invited to the 45th reunion coming up that summer. As things worked out, we were able to attend and it gave us an excuse to visit other family and connect with other old friends in and around Hendersonville and Asheville. After all, the mountains are the place to go in the summer when you live in Florida.

It seems the class had been having these reunions every five years since graduation and we all had a good time. I enjoyed meeting all my old friends, only some of whom I recognized. Most I wouldn't have known had I met them on a crowded street. In addition, I learned that a small group of about six or eight of the guys who I had been closest to in the Boy Scouts had been going camping for a long weekend every summer up in the mountains around Canton, usually on Mt. Pisgah where we used to go as kids. Oh, how I wish I knew they had been doing that! I would have made the effort to join them at least once in a while. At this point in their lives, the camping trip had evolved to a weekend at a very remote cabin one of them owned at the foot of Mt. Pisgah, and I did join them for the next three summer weekends. Unfortunately, Jerry has been very sick with cancer and the trips have stopped altogether. When anyone asks me what we did on those trips, I say, "We go for hikes, burn some steaks, drink beer, smoke cigars, sit around, tell stories, and lie to each other about our golf scores and the fish we caught."

Back to 2010. In the blink of an eye, five years went by and it was time for our 50th reunion, which, as far as I can tell will probably be the last big affair. I was standing around visitin' (as they say in the South) when three or four of the guys who I would consider my best friends, sort of cornered me and said they wanted to talk to me about something. Okay.

Them: "Joe, you're Jewish, right?"

Me, somewhat taken aback and flabbergasted: "Yes, of course, I assumed you always knew that."

Them: "Yeah, we guess we did, but we never really knew just what it was or what it meant."

Me: "Okay, well, what do you want to know."

Them: "Well, like every year right after school would start you were gone a few day for some kind of holiday; you got extra days off. We never knew what that was all about."

Me: "Didn't the teachers ever say anything? Didn't they tell you why I—we—were absent for two days?"

Them: "Nope, not a word. Just that you'd be out. You know, it wasn't until years later that I understood something about Jewish holidays and I realized what a teachable moment those teachers and the school system as a whole missed. Why do you suppose they let that pass them by? What do you suppose they were afraid of?"

Me: "Of course, I understand your point but I don't have an answer. We were given a note to give to the teacher, and some arrangement was made behind the scenes to give us the time off for the High Holidays – Rosh Hashanah and a week later Yom Kippur - and the opportunity to make up any missed schoolwork."

Them: "We always wondered about that. Another thing. About that bar mitzvah (he struggled with the words; I helped out) of yours we went to. How old were you?

Me: "Thirteen."

Them: "Well, you have to know we were very jealous of that whole thing." (I don't remember which of these guys were invited and/or attended but I know a few were and did, along with their families.)

Me: "Oh, why? How?"

Them: "How did you stand up there in front of that whole congregation and talk like that? I've thought of that my whole life. You spoke and read this strange language written in a whole different alphabet! Do you have any idea how amazing that was to us? We could never have done that."

Feeling pretty humbled I said, "I don't know what to say. It was just something that all Jewish boys learn to do. I started learning to read Hebrew about the same time I started learning to read English. The only difference is I understand English, but we were only taught to read Hebrew. We weren't taught to understand Hebrew, only to read it, which is really a shame because it is a really difficult language to learn and it would have been good to have learned at least some grammar and vocabulary.

"Now, I have a question for you guys. I've always been asked about what it was like growing up in a small southern town as the only Jewish family. Jews from the big city all think that I had to put up with a lot of anti-Semitism and prejudice. I never felt any. Did you know of such feelings in Canton? Did people talk about Jews, disliking Jews, not wanting to do business with us? Any of that sort of thing?

Them: "No, we pretty much never thought about it."

Whether that was an honest answer or not I'll ever know, but my experience of growing up in Canton leads me to believe that it was. I'm sure that Canton had its share of haters just like any town or group of people that you will find anywhere. After all, the town at that time was completely segregated. There was a water fountain on Main Street clearly marked white only and the bus station had segregated waiting rooms and the schools were strictly segregated between blacks and whites.

I asked my high school classmate, Llewellyn, whom I interviewed for this book, and asked her whether she was aware that I was Jewish. She wasn't, and that's so funny. "It meant nothing," she said. "I didn't have any concept of that, and it still doesn't bother me whether someone is Jewish or anything else. As prejudiced as my Dad was about black people, I'm surprised he didn't try to instill a prejudice about Jews. It was never talked about among the other kids."

When I asked her if she noticed when we were gone for the holidays, she just laughed and said, "We never even noticed you were gone."

My bar mitzvah

Learning from Dad at the store

The year before my bar mitzvah, Dad and I would lock the doors about five o'clock and sit behind the counter on stools where we would study the Torah. He taught me my portion, the weekly part that I would read on the Saturday of my bar mitzvah, he taught me to chant and he taught me the trope, the notes to chant. He taught me most of what I know; he also taught me to read Hebrew. It was a very special time.

Taller than the Rabbi

Then my other growth story, having to do with being so tall so young, that I've told everybody in the world was about my bar mitzvah. I was on the bimah—the raised platform in the front of the Synagogue where the rabbi conducts the service—and the rabbi was significantly shorter than me, and down under the bimah they had a small stepstool on which the normally shorter bar mitzvah boys would always stand when the rabbi was going to talk to them at the end of the ceremony, giving them their certificates, a gift or two, etc. In my case, the rabbi looked up at me, reached down and pulled out the stepstool, and he stood on it. He was a very small, older, very formal European rabbi. It makes me grin today thinking of the quiet laughter that rippled through the crowd at his expense. That's another one of those stories that you don't forget.

Two birthdays

Since turning 70 a couple of years ago, I have spent a lot of time looking back and thinking about what I consider to be the turning points in my life. While taking the memoir writing workshop in 2014 that led me to this book, our first assignment was to write about a branching point, in life, much like the turning points I'd been contemplating. I had no trouble defining what my first branch was, the subject of this story: my two birthdays.

I was born on October 17, 1942, but I didn't know that until the night of my bar mitzvah. I will assume that anyone reading this story has had some association in their lives with Jewish people and are aware that when a Jewish boy reaches his 13th birthday he enters adulthood from a religious perspective. This is normally the culmination of a number of years of study and then a great celebration and a party—which has gotten out of hand over my lifetime. These parties, in many cases, have gotten so big and so extravagant that they completely overwhelm the importance of the occasion. Incredible amounts of money are spent as families attempt to show each up and the children suffer the peer pressure of having these parties. All religious experience has become secondary to the party afterward.

So, here we were driving home from Asheville to Canton on the Friday night of my bar mitzvah, and as we approached the house my mother announced, in her most solemn and seldom used tone of voice, that she and Dad had something important to discuss with me. You see, up until that moment, and for every preceding year, my birthday had been celebrated on September 17, not October 17, and I had kind of wondered, but never asked the question why my bar mitzvah was on October 22. All my friends, including my older brother, had their bar mitzvahs on the weekend before or after their birthday. One didn't ask a lot in those days, one went with the flow; especially as I look back, the flow was pretty smooth and steady.

So, here we are, pulling into the driveway of the house on Pisgah Drive in Canton—the scene is indelibly etched in my memory—and my mother is telling me that a part of me is not what I thought it was. It was about a 40-minute drive and I'm still coming down from the adrenaline rush of the highest point of my young life, and now I'm trying to understand the words coming out of my mother's mouth.

What is she talking about? She's saying something about my birthday; it's October 17th. No, it's September 17. What? Why? What does this mean? My mind is in kind of a fog, I don't really want to deal with this, I want to know what's in these envelopes I've been handed, and the presents that are in the trunk, and she's telling me that my birthday has been on the wrong day. And so the conversation ended, for the time being.

It may not seem like a big deal, not knowing what day you are born on. Many cultures don't pay much attention to birthdays, but we're not other cultures, we're Americans, and to us birthdays are a big deal; an important part of our lives because we take pride in our personal growth, take stock of our lives and achievements through the years, things that are not emphasized in other countries. It was quite a shock, but there it was, get used to it; and so, I did. Still, every year when September 17 comes around, I tell my wife and anyone else, "Today is my other birthday."

As a famous radio personality, Paul Harvey used to say, "And now for the rest of the story." Why did my mother have to change my birthday? How did we come to be in Canton, NC in 1948? Was this really a major branching point in my life?

When thinking of writing about branching points, I realize that if this story is a main branch, then it can best be understood by describing other branches in my life; maybe a few twigs and couple of leaves thrown in before I'm done.

In 1945, two momentous, totally disparate, seemingly unrelated events occurred that came to have a direct bearing on my personal story. The biggest of which was the bombing of Japan by the world's first atomic bomb, which, ironically, saved my father's life. And the second was my Uncle Morris marrying Ann Williams of Hendersonville, NC. When you go to the library in Hendersonville, you pass the Morris Kaplan Auditorium, that's my uncle; a man of many more stories. Without him marrying Ann and coming to Hendersonville, my birthday wouldn't have gotten changed in Canton three years later.

Dad was an infantry private in the Army, stationed on an island in the Pacific Ocean with orders to be in the first wave to invade Japan in 1945 when the "bomb" was dropped on Hiroshima and Nagasaki. He was part of the American occupation in Tokyo and, soon thereafter, was discharged and sent home to Scranton, PA and his family. Then, however, it came about (a story that, sadly, I don't know in detail), his brother Morris convinced him to move his family down to North Carolina. Louis Williams, Morris' father-in-law, agreed to help Dad set up a business in Canton, and sometime in 1946 or '47 he opened Kay's Auto Parts on Main Street in Canton. Now, Canton in those days was a pretty miserable, backwater, smelly paper mill town of about 3,500 people. Why he went there instead of one of the other towns around the area, we never quite discovered.

There we were in Canton, a family of five. My older brother, Mort, me and our sister Judy and pretty soon along came Alan, so now there are four of us all under eight years old. My mother is pretty much alone, doesn't really know anyone—we are the only Jews in town so she doesn't have the opportunity to have church friends, they are in Asheville at the synagogue we joined. Asheville was a fairly long 25 miles away over a narrow, winding two-lane road at the time, and she didn't learn to drive for another five or six years. In addition to taking care of the four of us, she helped Dad in the store because she was a trained bookkeeper. That little twig or branch of this story is to try to get into her head and determine why she pushed up my birthday, or at least do my best to figure out why I think she did.

Birthday mystery solved

I was five going on six and had been in kindergarten for a year when the question arose about starting first grade. It turns out the cut-off for birthdays is—you guessed it—October 1. My mother must have decided that one less kid at home for six hours a day would be worth a little white lie, and what difference did a couple of weeks make anyway? Nobody knew much about child psychology or anything about the psychology of learning or the differences in learning between boys and girls. Nobody, at least in a place like Canton, paid much attention to the fact that most six-year-old girls are older than six-year-old boys in maturity and that being the youngest boy in a class is a really bad thing!

I was big for my age, really big, and for every year thereafter for that matter! Another twig off my branching point—maybe only a leaf—when I was born, my grandmother said she never saw an infant with such long, skinny arms, legs, fingers, and toes. She made my mother take me to the doctor because she was sure there was something wrong with me. She was right; when I was 13, I was 6 feet tall and wore size 13 shoes.

How did she get away with the lie? Mom's version of the story was that when she registered me for school they asked for proof of age, and she said that I didn't have a birth certificate. When they insisted on one, she made up a crazy story that her husband was in the Army in the Pacific and was going to invade Japan. When he asked for the children's birth certificates, they got lost in the Army bureaucracy. They insisted she write letters, etc. And so time passed without further questions. They let me en- roll anyway, Canton being a small town where everyone's honest you see. Soon, the birth certificate was forgotten about.

Thus, I was enrolled in first grade, a year ahead of my time. Looking back, I consider that to be the most significant branching point of my life. I was a terrible student throughout my academic career; barely surviving, disliking school, always feeling over my head and overwhelmed. It was always a struggle. Perhaps it is too easy to blame the fact that I should have waited another year to start. We'll never know. It wasn't until years later that I understood why all of my friends tended to be the kids a year or two behind me in school; why none of the girls in my class wanted to go out with me.

I did eventually complete college and obtained a Masters in Business Administration (MBA) from the Wharton School of Business at the University of Pennsylvania. But, it all came later in life, as an adult, when motivations are different.

Yogi Berra, the famous Major League Baseball player for the New York Yankees, was a master of malapropisms. One of my favorites quotes of his is, "When you come to the fork in the road, take it." Now, that may sound like nonsense, but I once met a friend of his who explained what he meant. Yogi lived on a large farm in northern New Jersey. The house was reached by a long driveway, and at one point you came to a fork in the road which was the beginning of a circular portion which went up to the front of the house. No matter which fork you took you ended up at the front door. Yogi always made perfect sense!

My point in telling this anecdote is to wonder if he really meant that in life we worry too much about the decisions we make. When we come to a decision point, make a decision and don't look back. Maybe either decision will work out in a positive way. I've tried to live by this idea: don't just stand there, do something, make a decision, move forward. If you're wrong, live with it, find a way to recover, learn from your mistakes but keep moving forward.

BBYO – AZA

The AZA is the boy's branch of the B'nai B'rith Youth Organization. All the Jewish kids in western North Carolina belonged to the Asheville chapter of BBYO. The boys to AZA and the girls to BBG – B'nai B'rith Girls. I say "all," but I'm sure there was someone out there who didn't want to associate with us, but I don't know who he or she was. If you wanted to be part of the teenage Jewish community, you joined BBYO and you were part of the group. There are other teenage youth groups to choose from as well. Each of the Synagogue organizations have competing groups, but in a town as small as Asheville there was really only room for one, at least at that time, so we all belonged to BBYO, AZA and I was an active member, or as active as I could be living in Canton.

Those of us who didn't live in Asheville had a built-in disadvantage which I alluded to earlier; we couldn't be there during the week for all the informal activities that went on so we missed a lot: ad hoc meetings that might go on in the school hallways, the day-to-day process of getting to know each other just because you were together all the time by default. When the only contact you have is a meeting that occurs on Sunday (how often were the meetings? I don't remember), the dances, and parties, etc., it becomes difficult to make and maintain friendships. And here, I must mention that the things that didn't exist to promote communication throughout the week. Phone calls were expensive. The only affordable way to communicate was to sit down and write a letter or send a post card to someone in the next town. Most of you reading this won't even know what a postcard is I'm afraid.

When I've talked to people from outlying towns such as Sylva and Hendersonville, they all tell the same story of being outwardly welcomed to the meetings and parties, but really feeling left out and treated like outsiders, never really included as part of the "in" group. I had a slightly better advantage in that we came to Asheville so regularly, were members of one of the synagogues and the Jewish Community Center, and participated in a lot of community activities. But as I look back, I believe that the only way to really be accepted and be part of a group of kids is to grow up with them in close proximity from the early grades on.

All of that aside, the BBYO was a good group, a good experience and we had a lot fun, especially after I moved to Asheville and could participate fully in everything that went on. There were chapters all over the country and all kinds of events and opportunities to meet kids from other places from other regions. The first regional event I remember going to was in Charlotte shortly after I got my driver's license; it became one of my favorite unforgettable stories, for me and my friends.

A volunteer was needed to drive to Charlotte, so guess who had just gotten his driver's license and wanted to show off. Believe it or not, my parents agreed to let me drive a car load of teenagers in our 1957 Cadillac, no adult supervision required, for a weekend BBYO event. What are the odds of that happening in today's world for a 16 year old? So off we go, six or seven kids; it was a big, big car and four in the back seat wouldn't have been uncomfortable. Off we went from Asheville to Charlotte, 1958, no Interstate 40 yet. I'm tooling along, driving through Hickory, radio blaring, oblivious to the speed limits, when all of a sudden I said, "Hey, what's that red light back there, and what's that siren sound?" Ooops! Big Ooops. We had cops chasing us! Uh, oh! Pull over.

"Son, where y'all think you're going so fast? Whose big Cadillac's this anyway? Where y'all from? Get outta this car and show me your driver's license."

Think I was scared? I was shaking so hard I couldn't get the door open. Try to explain to a country cop in Hickory, NC what a car load of Jewish kids were doing going to Charlotte to a convention of Jewish kids for the weekend when you're basically scared to death and the last time you dealt with a cop was when you got caught with firecrackers in Canton. The cop didn't make me call my father or anything from the road. He just gave me a ticket, a lecture, made sure we were all sober and he let us go. All weekend I had the burden of thinking about what would happen when I had to tell Dad what happened.

Anyway, I got written up for doing about 75 in a 45-mile-perhour zone. The worst thing was, Dad had to come back with me a month later to go to court and pay the fine. All the way back to Hickory! I don't recall if he made me pay for it; after all, what would I have used for money? All I had was what I made working in the store. It was nearly 40 years later and I was living in Florida before I got another speeding ticket.

AZA meetings were mainly about planning the next "event," a.k.a., party. About once a month there was some excuse to have a party with the BBG, the girls. The local girls, the Charlotte girls, the Greenville, SC girls, girls from somewhere. Hendersonville had the Jewish summer camps, Blue Star and Camp Judea (in those years I believe there was one other one), and we'd try to arrange events with them too, but the camps weren't crazy about doing that so it didn't happen too often. I did get introduced to Jewish girls, which was a good thing but never had a real Jewish girlfriend. First of all, none of them grew past 4'10", or so it seemed. As I've said over the years, God declared at some point that all Jewish girls born between about 1938 and 1950 would not be allowed to grow taller than 5'4", and in the tenth grade could not be taller than five feet tall. This seemed especially true if they lived anywhere in the southern United States.

As you now know, I was well over six feet tall, 130 pounds if I was lucky, awkward, socially somewhat inept, rhythmically challenged, and all the girls were way too short. I was one of those guys that was every- one's friend but no one's "boyfriend." I was also shy and afraid to ask girls out because they usually said no, and after a while…well you get the picture, enough of this. I didn't have many dates in those years. AZA was fun and a good experience in learning how to belong to an organization. We did a lot of activities, went to regional conventions and met a lot of people. It was the main focus of my social life in Asheville.

The new store
and more Canton stories

It's hard to blame parents for decisions they made. Actually, no, it's not hard; it's improper, it's wrong to blame. We all make the decisions in life that we have to make to support our family and ourselves. Those decisions are only wrong in retrospect; there are no do-overs in life. So Mom and Dad came to Canton for reasons that seemed to be the right ones for them at the time. They lived through the Great Depression, their grandparents must have lived through pogroms and wars. They must have known stories; they must have heard horrible stories. They must have lived through some horrible experiences, and Dad must have witnessed terrible events in the Far East in the islands during World War II.

I think they were afraid of city lifestyles. Mom was a small-town girl and Scranton was a small town, so they came here to Canton. I can only speculate what my life would have been like had they gone to Philadelphia with Bernie and Seymour. Had Dad become a rabbi, a college professor or an attorney, we would have grown up in the city and gone to Hebrew school and had a good Jewish education. Life is full of regrets, and while I look at the life I led growing up as I did, I also wonder about the missed opportunities that may have been afforded by growing up in the large cities of the northeast. I spent most of my adult life with Jews from Philadelphia, New York, Boston, and have heard their stories of what it was like to be in the majority in the neighborhood, in school, to not have to be constantly explaining who you were. All the girls were Jewish, most of the food was kosher. What would that life have been like? How would I have been different? Or would I?

The small store on Main Street met with some success over the years. Dad worked hard and became well-regarded in town. He joined local civic organizations and I believe he was on the Canton City Council. He got involved with local churches and was friends with various Christian ministers. He was invited to teach on Sundays, so we were part of the community and everyone knew the Kaplan kids. I don't know if his teaching was at his instigation or the ministers invited him as a result of their getting to know him. I suspect that Dad and the more open-minded clergy became friends, discussed religion and philosophy, and out of those relationships invitations were forthcoming to teach a class or give a lecture. Perhaps it was well received, the people were interested and one thing led to another. Dad was also interested in teaching about Judaism; he was well-versed in Torah and Bible and I'm sure that is what he taught. Whether he ever engaged in heated discussions or

arguments I have no idea but it would not have been his style to get into arguments with other people. I don't know that I ever remember him raising his voice to anyone over anything.

At some point he decided to build a new store and he had an eye on a lot up the street from the current Kay's Auto Parts location. The problem was, the lot was a mountain. After all, we lived in the mountains and everything was comprised of hills and mountains. It was beautiful there, of course, except for the damn mill. We didn't know that as kids—the leaves changed every fall and we didn't realize the beauty of it. People come up to these mountains in autumn to delight in the change of season. In October, the tourists come and pay lots of money to rent mountain cabins and fill our local Bed and Breakfast homes just to watch the leaves change. To us, it was just another regular experience in our lives.

In school every fall, one of our projects was to go out and collect the many colored leaves and paste them into workbooks. We would collect as many different kinds and sizes and colors as we could find and then learn the names: beautiful red maples which turned a bright, fiery red, dogwood, cherry, poplars, and oaks, which dropped their acorns and we'd watch the squirrels gather them up, stuffing them in their checks as fast as possible and running to hide them. We supposedly could predict the winter weather by how heavy the acorn crop was, the more acorns the colder it was going to be. The leaves would crinkle and break as they dried out and we pasted them in the pages. What did we use? Elmer's Glue®? Or did we just mix up flour and water? Or LePage's Glue® in the bottle with the rubber top that always got stuck? Don't remember. But we'd put the leaves on that cheap lined paper and carefully print the names under each one and then bind the pages together, punching holes and maybe tying them with a colored string into a book, the whole project smelling of fall and getting ready for Thanksgiving with a cutout picture of a big turkey on the front.

Back to Dad, he had his eye on this mountain that he envisioned could be a suitable location for the new and improved auto parts store, plus he wanted a big garage for a machine shop and to be able to repair cars and trucks. Everybody told him he was crazy. They said, "Kay, you cain't dig down that thar mountain." They assumed that the street above it would collapse and bring with it the house that "set up thar" (in the local vernacular) that belonged to the owner of the paper mill. But, Dad had a stubborn vision. I don't know who he talked to, or how he did it, but he dug out that mountain and built Kay's Auto Parts. In today's language, he likely got an option on the land. He went to the bank and he talked the bank into making a loan or perhaps giving him a commitment for financing; after all, it was small-town America in the 1950s and agreements were bound with handshakes and the bank loaned its own money. Lending money was very personal in those days.

Somehow, Dad heard about someone who owned a gigantic steam shovel. Apparently, it was the largest piece of equipment of its kind that anybody in those parts had ever seen or heard of. Dad arranged to have it brought to Canton and he determined

to have all that dirt removed to cut down that mountain. And so he did. I guess I was 10 or 11 years old at the time and I don't remember watching it work, but I must have stood there as a little boy after school and watched that thing reduce the mountain to a plot of flat land. Loading the trucks, one great big shovelful at a time, and eventually that mountain was gone.

I had friends that lived up on the street above the mountain when it was still a mountain. We used to walk down to Main Street below along a trail well-worn by the feet of boys as well as adults. Needless to say, we felt that Dad was taking our trail away. It wasn't just a barren old hill. It had trees and weeds and secret places for kids to play, so Dad was destroying our little slice of mountainous heaven. The street above was kind of a loop; that street led to another street, forming a loose sort of connection from one side of town to the other. In this trail, we had what was to us a secret shortcut from the houses on the street above down to town without having to walk all the way around. That was soon to disappear forever in one act of small-town development.

Other than us kids, the whole town was excited about what Kay was doing. He sure changed the town because the fact is what Dad was doing was right in the center of town. Canton only had two streets. Let me describe for you the pleasure of going to Canton, smelling the sweet smoke of the sulfur that's still coming out of those smokestacks. Sixty years later, they've cleaned it up quite a bit.

You'll be interested to know that Champion Paper and Fibre Company was, I believe, the number one U.S. Environmental Protection Agency's Superfund cleanup site when America finally decided to clean up its environment. Sometime early in the 20th century, the owner of the mill decided that the Pigeon River would be a good place to build a paper manufacturing company because it was surrounded by thousands of acres of forest, and you need lots of trees to make paper. You also need a lot of flowing water to operate a successful paper mill. So, the Pigeon River in Canton became the prime resource for Champion, which owned the town; it was truly the only reason the town was there.

Canton became one of the many places across post-World War II America that became known as a "company town." Have you ever heard of a company town? The mill was huge. I don't know many acres it covered but in a town with population variously stated, in the years we lived there, as between 4,000 and 5,000, the mill, at its peak of operation employed over 3,000 people. It had its own police force, railroad, logging crews (at least in the early years), and electrical generating capacity. In 1920 it built a YMCA for its employees that became the center of social life for generations of employees and their children. Every possible activity was provided there.

And then there was the company store which opened in 1926 to offer groceries and other dry goods to mill employees. It was supposed to function much like a general store. Except that the employees were paid in scrip—a form of legal tender used in lieu of money and a common practice in cash-poor, remote locations where one employer dominated. Scrip (also called chits

or vouchers) was given to employees of the company as credit against their wages. Employees were expected, nearly forced, to buy everything they could from the company store. This made employees, their families, and entire communities completely dependent on the company. Scrip was not the same as cash and was not accepted anywhere outside the company store, except for a few businesses in the community, like my father, who understood the desperation of our neighbors and occasionally accepted scrip in lieu of cash. When we arrived in 1946, employees were still being paid largely in scrip and it continued for years.

If you drove from Asheville to Canton, you came in on old route 19/23. Old 19/23, was a narrow, curving, dangerous two-lane road which we drove back and forth to and from Asheville innumerable times. I remember one section in particular: Driving toward Asheville, the road, all at once, went up a hill around a sharp curve and over a bridge. I remember Dad teaching us a life lesson, he said, "Now, boys, you remember that whenever there's a stretch of road that goes up a hill, around a curve, and over bridge, there's always going to be a car coming in the other direction." That was our first driving lesson, and I've remembered it all my life, because it's true; there's always a car coming in the other direction on a bad stretch of road like that. I shared that same wisdom with my children when they were learning to drive and if they read this, I hope they'll remember it. When you return from Asheville to Canton, just as you get to the town line, you come to Canton Hill. Now whether that's the official name on any map you may find I have no idea, I've never looked. But ask anyone in Haywood County and they'll tell you, you have to go up Canton Hill to get to Canton.

The Mile Straight

First, here's a little sidebar. Before you get to Canton Hill, you come to what was called, The Mile Straight. If you drive along the old 19/23, it's still there, but you have to know how to find it today. The Mile Straight was part of that narrow, curvy, dangerous mountain road, so to have a perfectly straight, flat, one-mile piece of road was an interesting phenomenon. At that time, in the late 1940s and early '50s, there were guys coming back from the war and they had a little money in their pockets. Combine scarcity with moonshiners running moonshine out of the hills and a lot of teenagers who wanted to show off, you end up with quite a show on the Mile Straight. Young men would soup up their cars—or pay us to do it for them—and that marked the momentous beginning of dirt track racing and, most people don't know it, but the beginning of NASCAR.

Everybody needed a place to go to see who had the fastest, hottest car. With a straight run of highway right here in Canton and not much else to do for entertainment, what do you think was going on every Saturday night? The Mile Straight became a very popular venue for car racing. Sadly, a lot of cars got totaled, spectators got injured, and kids got killed on the Mile Straight. It was a seemingly irresistible adrenaline rush that brought with it the momentary thrill of speed and often, a lasting pain of loss time and again. It was a quintessential American pastime.

One more story about the Mile Straight. After Dad built the new building equipped with a regular garage and full-time mechanics rebuilding engines, they needed a place to take the rebuilt engine to test it. So they would take it out there on the Mile Straight because it was only a couple of miles from our garage. They'd rev it up and see how fast they could get each gear going at top speed. There wasn't any place else you could run it for a whole mile and get up any speed in the mountains.

A lot of engines were laid to rest on that stretch of road, but only one that blew up under Dad's driving—Morty's car, but that's a different story.

Getting back to Canton. You must resist the urge to see how fast you can go coming down The Mile Straight and round a couple more curves before you reach the base of Canton Hill. I don't know how long that hill is, I suppose it's another mile before you get to the top of the incredibly steep grade. Almost as soon as you reach the top of the hill, you can nearly coast down a few feet right into town and right past Kay's.

The Canton Hill was good for business. It was a good thing for the Kaplan's resulting from a bad thing that happened to many drivers coming up that hill. A lot of old trucks tried to haul too many logs up that hill to the paper mill and broke down. Their engines ran fine on a straightaway or up and down more moderate mountain grades, but they weren't built to haul weight up that hill. But by the time they reached the top of Canton Hill—if they reached the top—they couldn't make the grade so to speak. And they'd walk or hitchhike up to Kay's Auto Parts, come into the store telling the all-too-familiar story, "Kay, my truck broke down on the hill, could you come down to get it started?" And either Dad or myself plus one of the mechanics would go down to see what needed to be done. We would eventually get the truck into the garage and rebuild an engine, install a new starter, replace a broken axle, or fix whatever it needed to get the trucks running again. We didn't always service trucks: old cars broke down just as often trying to get up that hill. Then there was wintertime. Imagine what a little snow or ice did to thwart travel up Canton Hill. It didn't take much to stop traffic.

Every year in the late fall we'd get a big truckload of tire chains to see our customers through another winter. Another of my trained skills was learning how to install tire chains on big trucks. I have memories etched in my mind—like getting frostbite from lying on my back in the freezing snow, in the pitch black dark, on the side of the road on Canton Hill— other trucks and cars struggling and slipping sideways to get past us— installing tire chains! My fingers were instantly stinging cold against the frozen steel of the chains as I tried to manipulate the little hooks that held the chains in place around the back side of the big truck tires where you can't see what you were doing. I can still feel the cold.

As you come up the hill there's a light at the top. As you drive through the light you start down the much gentler slope and the street splits three ways—Main Street to left, Park Street to the right, and a sharp right down to the mill. As a kid, I never knew the names of any of the streets in town. They were just there and we all innately knew which way to go when we wanted to get someplace in our little mountain-top corner of the world. It was almost as though we were born with the map in our heads. Who needs street names when you just go "that way?"

Childhood was made of streets like these

Main Street was home to most of the shops. Park Street took you down to the post office, the bus station, and a little café called Charlie's. Both streets continued down to the Little Pigeon River, which in those days was a pretty ugly sight to behold most of the time because of the mill's discharge polluting and ruining the river. This is where the bridge was built that crossed the river and from which the town took its name as the steel for the bridge came from Canton, OH. We walked across that bridge every day going to and from high school and would look down at the river and see these big, floating blobs of brownish, white foamy stuff pretty much filling the river as far down river as we could see. It looked something like dirty soap scum piled high, and it killed the fish down river as far as Tennessee for years and years until the 1970s when they were finally forced to clean it up.

Park Street and Main Street both went across the river and then joined together again to become route 23 which took you out of town to Clyde, NC, which is about five miles away.

Let's back up: when you come over the hill to that main intersection where the streets split at the light, the new store is on your left, and when we lived there you could bear left and drive down Main Street. Now it is a one-way street coming up, but if you ignore the one-way and go down Main Street past the store, the first left turn is Academy Street, and our first house is the third house on the left opposite the big Baptist Church. Main Street looks pretty much the same as when we left in 1957, different businesses, but same store fronts. Time has pretty much passed Canton by, sad to say. Someone who hasn't been there in a long time can pick out the subtle changes—a missing building here, a new storefront there—but all in all it looks the same. A major change was the missing garage building in the back of the store that Dad had built. No one I talked to recently knew it had ever been there so they didn't know when it was torn down.

Walking up Academy Street, the only difference is the house on the lot between our house and Shulman's house, otherwise everything is exactly the same. The trowel marks my uncle or grandfather made on the wall are still there, the steps they built beside the driveway are exactly as they left them, the brick siding is as Dad built it. I even knocked on the door and went inside and very little had changed. It was a very weird feeling, a real time warp.

Back on the corner of Main and Academy is the three-story yellow brick building that housed the pharmacy downstairs and Dr. Westmoreland's office upstairs. He was my doctor as a little boy, the one I liked. Walking into his office, you walked down a short hall to Mrs. Allen sitting behind a glass window who always greeted everyone with a cheer- ful hello and checked you in and sent you to the waiting room which was always full of patients of every age and description. (I never realized she was my buddy Jerry's mother.) I came in multiple times, often carried by a frantic parent, bleeding from one extremity or another to be sewn up once again by the patient and invariably calm and reassuring Dr. Westmoreland. Morty and I even had our tonsils removed in his office, and I remember him prescribing ice cream and milk shakes as Dad carried us out of the office and up the hill to recover at home.

About 1970, my wife, Sue, and our son, Dan, came back to visit Hendersonville, and I took them to see Canton. I went up to see if Dr. Westmoreland was still there, and sure enough, Mrs. Allen was still sitting there behind the glass window. I asked her if she recognized me, and after a minute she did. She went to ask the doctor if he could see me as the office was still full of what appeared to be the same people as when I was last there all those years ago. We sat and talked for a few minutes; he seemed as unchanged as the town and pleased that I remembered him and took the time to stop by and say hello. He died a few years later, I'm not sure exactly when. He probably died too young because he never stopped smoking.

The interest of money

Across Main Street was the bank. I think it was the only bank in town, and it was where I learned about banking, making deposits for the store, getting change, and most importantly saving money. It has always surprised me, the little things that I realize I know, that seem obvious and second nature, as a result of growing up in a family business. For instance, I always knew that at the end of the day or every couple of days all the money that came in had to be deposited in the bank, checks had to be endorsed on the back, deposit slips had to be filled out, all the transactions had to be entered in journals, everything had to add up and balance. I was so surprised to learn that they had courses in college to teach people those things, with tests and exams. Professors taught it in ways to make it difficult and I thought about how simple it all was to a 12-year-old boy whose mother showed it all to him, and sent him off to the bank with the day's deposit.

I also learned about saving money at that bank. You see, I got paid for all that work I did at the store. I didn't get an allowance, I got a paycheck. I think I started at either 50 cents or 75 cents per hour and over the years moved up the scale. But there was a kicker; half of everything I earned went into a passbook savings account at the bank. At first this didn't seem fair, it seemed like a punishment. After all, I wanted that money for movies and candy and, and, well, I needed that money. But after a while I started paying attention to the numbers in that passbook and I started to notice that every once in a while they added a little something to it—a very little something called interest. It was only a few pennies but it was there. I hadn't done anything for it except put my money in there, and lo and behold they gave me more money. Now this started to get interesting. So, over the years I kept adding to that passbook, and as it added up I never, ever took anything out because I realized how hard I had to work to put that money in there. I didn't close that account until I went off to college, to George Washington University in 1962. All that work, starting at 50 cents an hour turned into over $500, which was a lot of money for college in those days when tuition was charged in the tens of dollars, not thousands.

On down Main Street, cross the old steel bridge that the town was named for, and turn left and go a few blocks to the Canton High School. The football stadium is still across the street from the high school and also on that side of the street is the little league field where I learned that I was afraid of the baseball when the pitcher threw it at me as hard as he could and I was supposed to stand there and try to hit it. Also, there is the city swimming pool where I learned to swim, a couple of clay tennis courts where I learned to play tennis, and the softball stadium. The mill sponsored a semi-pro, men's fast-pitch softball team. That was a great game to watch and Canton had a great team in those years; a championship team with a great pitcher who went by the awful name of Nazi Miller. We always went to the games, and at one point I even worked in the stand selling concessions such as peanuts and popcorn.

If you went down past the mill, North Main Street took you up another mountainside to North Canton where there was another residential area. I never ventured up to that part of Canton and never had friends that lived on that side of town.

When Dad excavated his lot and built the new store, he drove everybody in town crazy because of the audacity of such an undertaking. The building that Dad built is a two-story yellow
brick building. In design it is not very architecturally interesting, very plain and utilitarian. The ground floor was divided into two halves with one half being Kay's Auto Parts and the other half rented to Dr. Kearse. I don't know what the dimensions were, how large the lot was, certainly not more than half an acre, or how large the store was. As you faced the store you would see glass front windows with a door in the center and a driveway to the right. The whole right side was also glass windows with another door on the right with parking beside the building. A customer coming in the front door would walk 6 or 10 steps to the front counter which was probably 10 feet long, maybe more, and the space from the door to the counter would have merchandise displays such as cases of motor oil, tires, tire chains, tools, wall displays, large signs, and sales materials of various kinds. There were four rows of shelves behind the counter filled with inventory of auto parts. At the right end of the counter, as you faced it, the counter turned the corner and in the corner Mom had her desk and did the bookkeeping. Mom and Dad were frugal and didn't believe in wasting money on niceties such as office space. After all, you couldn't wait on customers from an office. From the last row of shelves on the right to the side of the building there was a wide space, maybe 10 or 15 feet, that was used for a variety of things including a walkway to the back door and out to the garage in back. Over the few years of its existence, those front and side spaces were used to display and sell everything from International Harvester Trucks and Tractors to Briggs and Stratton lawn mowers. It was also used by Dad to rebuild engines, lawnmowers, kids' bicycles, and anything else that came along. In the back was the glass shop and a large storage area filled with items such as automobile tail pipes, axles, the glass inventory, and other miscellaneous stuff.

Next door, downstairs, as I said was Dr. Kearse, a general practitioner who I was forced to see from time to time much to my displeasure. Billy was my best friend. The Kearse family lived down the block from us on Johnson Street and Billy Kearse and I played together practically every day. He was the oldest of four children and his mother was a really nice lady who took good care of us. When she was pregnant with her fourth child, it was summer and she couldn't get around much, so she invited us in and taught us all how to play bridge. It's sad and confusing when children become aware that not everyone is kind, especially adults in your community whom you should otherwise trust. I think Dr. Kearse was mean to his wife. I think he beat her and the kids, so I didn't much like that. Back then, you minded your own business and didn't talk about such things, but were bothered, just under the surface, believing as though disturbed by some indefinable evil. But he was our tenant, and I assume he helped pay the mortgage.

Upstairs were offices rented to various people including an alcoholic dentist, another one of those undiscussed evils. I recognized as a child that the dentist was a drunk, but we were seemingly stuck with that situation too. I told my mother I thought he was drinking, that he smelled of whiskey, but the rent had to be paid, I suppose. I have a vague memory of telling my mother that I thought there was something wrong with him but being told that we had to keep going to him. I remember being relieved when we finally moved to Asheville and had to find new doctors and dentists. Another tenant was our accountant, a Hungarian immigrant, a children's psychiatrist who my mother insisted was crazier than any of his patients and from whom I got my initial cynicism about such people. And I believe a hair dresser perhaps.

On the back half of the lot Dad built a simple cinderblock garage with a great big, two-story garage door with an electric garage-door opener with one of those steel boxes with a big red button on top and a green one on the bottom. The garage was big enough to park an 18-wheel tractor-trailer, a school bus, or other big trucks. There was a space between the two buildings with a little parking lot. About nine parking spaces were painted and you could fit them all in if you parked the cars side-by-side and bumper-to-bumper. Guess who was responsible for fitting as many cars as possible into that lot? I learned to drive by moving those cars around. I'll tell you about that in a minute. After all was said and done, the building got built, the offices got rented, business came regularly and the store was busy. The garage was particularly busy; dad hired mechanics to manage the workload. The Korean War ended in 1953, and the economy started to pick up, people started to have money. I recall we employed a young man back from Korea as a mechanic who told us stories of the war.

As I got older I went to the store every day after school. Soon, I was mature enough to stand up behind the counter and take care of customers—I'd say I was big enough, but height always beat me to the finish line as I was rarely as mature as you'd expect from someone as tall as me.

Let me back up and tell you a story about Billy's mother and one of the neat things she did—it's one of my favorite stories. When we were 12 years old and starting seventh grade, there were four or five of us and she said she'd drive us all to school the first day of school. She was a nurse and must've known that it was about that time, we'd all experience a growth spurt. She said, "Everybody come to my house and I'll drive you kids to school." So we all went to her house on the designated morning and she said, "Now, before you go to school I'm going to measure all of you guys; next year I'll measure you again and we'll see who grows the most." Well, I measured just about five feet that year. The next year, she couldn't reach the top of my head. She was a little woman, so she dragged over an old wooden chair, hopped up on it and measured my height. I was just over six feet. I remember very clearly her having to get on a chair and making a big deal of it. Obviously, it wasn't a big surprise as we saw each other practically every day as Billy and I were together constantly and everyone could practically see me growing. I remember growing remarkably fast that year, 1955. I remember buying a pair of shoes for Rosh Hashanah. There was a men's clothing store on Main Street just a few stores down from our store, I think it was Winner's. Mom and I went down there to buy a pair of shoes. My feet were pretty big and the owner of the store measured my feet. I remember my mother being distressed because she had to buy her 12-year-old boy a man-size shoe, size 12. To add insult to injury, I think they were a whopping $20. I wore them for the high holidays that year— Rosh Hashanah, Yom Kippur and Sukkot—put them away in the closet and didn't try them on again until the next holiday. By then, as you might have guessed, they already didn't fit. That was not a happy time because I went from a size 12 to 13 in less than a year and another pair of $20 shoes and there was nothing to be done about except to pray that at some point my feet would stop growing. Luckily they did finally, at size 14, but by then I was buying shoes with my own money.

I've wandered off of the new store stories, so let's go back and see where I was. Dad started teaching me to drive when I was about 12. This was about the time I began parking the cars in the lot at Kay's. There really wasn't much teaching involved as I grew up surrounded by cars all the time. I just sort of got behind the wheel and drove. I was big enough to be behind the wheel before puberty and could reach the pedals with ease. I was playing with real cars from the time I was 11 or 12. Dad let me move the cars around, start them up, and drive them a few feet every now and then, but when we moved into the new building, there was all this space back there. The mechanics would let me get behind the wheel of the cars and trucks when they were working on an engine. They'd be under the hood or under the car and they would need somebody to be in the car to start the engine or to do some other task, and I always liked to be there to help them. By the time I was 13, I was driving them in and out of the garage and moving them around. Those who rented office space in the building parked their cars in our lot. They had to park their cars bumper-to-bumper and very close, side-by-side, so there was just enough space for them to open their doors and pull their cars out. When someone got out of work, their car was, more often than not, blocked in by the other cars. Cars would have to be moved out of the way to extract their particular vehicle, and since people tended to get out of work after I arrived at the store after school, I was the person who moved the cars. As a result, I learned to back cars out of very tight spaces. I don't think I ever scratched one, because if I had, I probably would've lost my job. I learned a trick so I could drive as often as possible and experience the thrill of the challenge of moving those cars around: I learned who got out of work first and made sure their car was blocked by the most cars so I could do the most driving.

From the 8th grade through the 10th, I worked in the store almost every day after school and I loved every minute of it. I certainly liked being at work more than I liked being at school. When one uses the modern psychological jargon; phrases like "bonding with one's father," that certainly is what I did and what he did with me. I worked on the counter, sold merchandise, put away inventory, and stocked inventory. I helped Mom with the books and I moved the cars around. I worked with the mechanics, went out on the road and loaded up the trucks with merchandise. I knew how to run an auto parts store by the age of 15. What I didn't do was study very much and I didn't make very good grades.

It must have been a good business for a few years because we lived pretty well in Canton compared to what a lot of my friends had. I'm sure there were some doctors and lawyers in town who had a lot more money and possessions than we did, but there were a vast majority of people who had an awful lot less. We had a nice house always drove nice cars. Dad insisted on driving Cadillacs or Buicks. His cars were always two years old when he bought them. He had a deal with Harry Blomberg in

Asheville— there was Dad, always looking for the deal. Harry's Cadillac was still there in 2015. Having new cars frequently was great for us, but must of been kind of ostentatious. Mort and I still talk about why Dad insisted on driving those big Cadillacs in that little town. I don't think we ever heard any comments from anyone, but we felt kind of funny.

We took vacations. We went to Miami a couple of times and to Philadelphia, where Dad's family was. We never wanted for anything. We were never hungry; the pantry was always full. Mom had household help in Ella Mae and Zora Bell. Ella Mae claimed to be half Cherokee, and Zora Bell was her daughter. Ella Mae cleaned and cooked and Zora Bell would babysit at night when Mom and Dad would go to Asheville. I remember that Zora Bell was mean and would hit us if we didn't behave. We would tease her and hide and do what little boys did to make trouble, so her hitting us didn't stop us it seems.

Ironically, the business lasted until the economy got better after the Korean War. Eisenhower started building highways, enabling more people to travel, and they started being able to afford new cars instead of fixing their old ones. The old 19/23 Highway was straightened out and expanded to a three-lane highway, which is still the highway that you can take today. Of course, today you can take I-26, which conveniently, and totally, bypasses Canton. You really have to want to go to Canton to get to Canton. It's not as easy as driving through Canton to get someplace else. So, with more money in the economy, greater mobility, and better roads, people didn't need stores like Kay's Auto Parts. Things we sold could be bought cheaper at Sears and K-mart or in the better stores in Asheville. People stopped fixing things and instead replaced old cars with new ones.

In 1958, Dad sold the buildings and bought a similar business in Asheville, the Asheville Battery Company. I remember people telling Dad when he built that building in Canton that he should put an engraved concrete or stone or other marker that read Kaplan Building up on top so the building would forever be known as his. Dad, being Dad, was too modest and he refused to do it. Instead, he just put a little temporary sign attached to the building, which of course disappeared fairly quickly after we left. So now no one knows who built the building or when or why, but it's still there and doesn't look its age. The concrete block garage in back is long gone. I have no idea when it was torn down and the few people I have asked about it didn't know it was ever there. Shortly after Dad sold the building and bought the new business, we left Canton and moved to Asheville.

There was a moment of indecision before we left Canton when everything had been sold but nothing had been bought when Mom and Dad called a family meeting. I recall all six of us sitting around the dining room table and them being very serious, telling us what was going on. I suppose only Morty and I were really old enough to understand, but they laid the situation out to us. The house on Pisgah Drive was sold, the store building was sold. We had picked out a very nice house in Asheville that we all liked but it hadn't been bought yet. Dad was working on buying a business in Asheville but no deal had been made and the plan was to keep Kay's Auto Parts in Canton for another year so Morty could finish high school in Canton and I could finish 10th grade and play one more year of JV basketball. Dad and Mort and I would commute from Asheville every day. Also, Dad was buying a gas station in West Asheville as another business. Or not. Should we not do any of this? There was a sizable sum of money in the bank. I have no idea how much; I don't think they told us, but enough.

Should we not do any of this and instead move back to Philadelphia? Seymour and Bernie were starting to be successful in the home construction business they had started in Willow Grove, PA. Should we go back up there and go into business with them? Or go back up there and find some other business to invest in? Were the opportunities better in

Philadelphia than in Asheville? What a decision! Talk about branching points! We were, of course, too young to begin to understand how to analyze the situation and help make the decision and I don't know how they went about making the decision to stay in Asheville and buy Asheville Battery Co. which is what they did. And I'm not going to pass judgment here with the wisdom of hindsight. Because, as I said earlier, they made the decision they felt they had to make.

Dad in front of newly built Kay's Auto Parts
Main St., Canton, NC circa 1952

Cars and Trips

Dad was a car guy, he loved cars. He loved buying them, trading them, fixing them, taking them apart. But most of all he loved driving them. He loved getting the whole family in the car and going for a drive. He loved the big old cars built in the 1950s, Buicks, and Pontiacs, and Cadillacs. Cars big enough for the six of us to travel in comfortably, three in the front and three in the back.

There was always a competition for who got to sit in the front with Mom and Dad and who was stuck in the back in the middle seat. Initially, it was decided by who got there first, which resulted in races to the car and some all out brawls and lots of tears. Mort, being the oldest, figured riding shotgun should be his privilege, but that didn't last long. After all, I was soon bigger than him. Mom, being the peacemaker, came up with a system that lasted for a number of years. She kept a journal in the glove compartment and here's how it worked: Whenever anybody went anywhere in the car, no matter how long or how short a trip and no matter who else went along, if they sat in the front seat they had to enter their name in the log along with the time and date. They then went to the bottom of the list and it was the next one's turn.

This system worked fine until it was time to go on a major trip. More rules were needed. As I recall, the rules went something like this: Whoever's turn it was when we started out went first and had the front seat for the first 250 miles. It wasn't unusual for a major trip to begin at 4:30 or 5:00 am, but that's just the luck of the draw, after which it was the next person's turn. I'll tell you about our trips, but suffice it to say that Dad never stopped. So, whenever the odometer hit 250 miles, the change occurred by climbing over the seat into the back and the next one climbing into the front. There were no seat belts or child seats in those days keeping us legally bound to our current spot. It could be the middle of the night with everyone asleep, but Mom or Dad had to wake up whoever was next up front, or there would be hell to pay. That front seat privilege was sacrosanct.

Vacation Trips

We usually took one major vacation a year in December because school was out for two weeks for what was then known as the Christmas break. We went in one of two directions, either to Miami or to Philadelphia, as they were equidistant from Canton, about 18 to 20 hours of almost non-stop driving, and Dad did all the driving. However, before the last Miami trip, Mort had turned 16 and had his driver's license, so he was allowed to do some of the driving. When I say we rode almost non-stop, I mean that Dad only reluctantly stopped for gas. The usually response to, "I've got to go really, really, really bad," was, "Open a window." I don't think any of us ever actually opened a window and attempted that maneuver, although I wonder what they would have done if we'd had the nerve to try.

I don't remember my grandparents riding all the way to Florida with us, as that would have been eight of us in the car which doesn't seem possible. They may have taken the train to Miami for the winter and met us there.

I assume the budget was tight, and there weren't many motels/ hotels along the road in those days anyway, but the biggest problem was eating.

You see, we kept kosher, really kept kosher. Therefore, Mom brought almost everything that we ate; there were no restaurant meals allowed, so there was no need to stop except for gas and toilets. We could buy snacks such as sodas and candy bars, but no real food. We were loaded up with cold roast chicken, tuna salad, salami, bread, cheese, and I don't remember what else, but there was plenty.

The decision of where to go was a tough one and usually changed from minute to minute as the day for leaving approached. One time, the decision was made to go to Miami, so Mom packed for the six of us, Dad loaded the car, and off to bed we went with plans to get up about 5:00 am and hit the road. The getting up part went off on schedule. But Dad's mom lived in Philadelphia, and when he woke up, he decided that he felt like visiting his mother instead of going to Florida. So here we are at 5:00 am unloading the car, unpacking the suitcases, finding winter clothes, repacking, and eventually heading out to chilly Philadelphia instead of the sunshine and beaches of warm Miami. Actually, we weren't going to Philadelphia, we were going to Uncle Seymour's house in Willow Grove, PA, a suburb north of Philadelphia. Mom suggested we call Uncle Seymour and Aunt Shirley and let them know we were on the way, but Dad nixed that idea, he liked surprises. They had a big house and four kids of their own, so what if six relatives dropped in unannounced? Would you mind? As things turned out, given traffic, getting lost, etc.—remember this all predates interstate highways, cell phones, and GPS devices—we finally pulled in about 4:00 or 5:00 am the next day. The major advancement in those days was the addition of the Baltimore Harbor Tunnel. We *always* got lost going through Baltimore, so the tunnel was a great excitement although, as I recall we still got lost going through Baltimore.

When we finally arrived, everyone in the house was asleep, but the doors were unlocked—this was a different era, remember my theme of growing up free. We all went in quietly, found a couch or chair or space on the floor and went to sleep. At some point, the first uncle or aunt or cousin woke up and came downstairs, a few excited screams and *ohmygodswhatareyoudoinghere* and the rest is history. We had a nice visit despite us being surprise visitors, although I'm not sure Aunt Shirley ever forgave her brother-in-law for that one.

The reason Miami was the other destination of choice was the kosher hotels that were still in existence at the time. I believe they were located in what is now the very fashionable South Beach area. I remember them being rather small hotels, a couple of blocks back from the beach. There were also kosher restaurants and delis, at least one of which may still be there. The Miami trips were fun, and I remember the last one took place when Morty was 16, because he got to drive, as he now had his driver's license. I wonder how that affected the front seat rotation? Hmmm.

What I remember about visiting the Atlantic Ocean in Miami, are the jelly fish, which kept us out of the water most of the time we were there, and getting sunburned. Dad wasn't into boating or fishing or any such sports, in fact he never participated or was interested in any sports. About all I remember is the huge beaches, the palm trees, playing in the surf, the big deli menus, and the small hotels. I remember walking up Collins Avenue and looking at the big, expensive resort hotels, some of which are still there, such as the Fontainebleau and the Dunes. We would sometimes venture into the grand lobbies and dare to walk around and look at how the other people lived. Then, we would be back in the car for our drive back to Canton.

I have no idea what we did all day for what must have been 7 or 10 days, but I guess it was fun. I wonder if my parents ever thought about moving there? So many Jews from up north went there on vacation in those days, decided the climate was so much nicer, and never went back to the cold. It certainly would have been nicer than growing up in Canton.

Those were the only real vacations we had, but we took a lot of Sunday drives. We had picnics up in the mountains on the Blue Ridge Parkway to Mount Pisgah and Mount Mitchell, as well as trips to Murphy and Sylva, Hiwassee Dam, Lake Junaluska, and all over Western North Carolina, usually with at least two or three other families. Mom and Dad loved to pile all of us in the car and take off for the day and drive up in the mountains. The only one who really didn't like to go was Judy, who always got carsick. No one had any real sympathy for her because none of us understood that she was really sick, I guess.

Though Dad loved his cars, he never got involved with racing or the people who built cars for racing, although he had the opportunity. As I mentioned earlier, not many people know that the beginnings of NASCAR occurred here in the mountains and actually started with men building fast cars to run moonshine out of the hills ahead of the revenuers. A famous 1950s movie, Thunder Road, starring Robert Mitchum about moonshine in the mountains, was filmed in Asheville. Dad actually built a car for one of the these moonshine runners by taking a Cadillac engine and putting it in one of the smallest cars of the era, a Henry J—which no one reading this probably ever heard of—and making a vehicle consisting of basically an engine and a tank to hold the liquor. He also built cars for a couple of the very early race car drivers who ran on the first dirt track in Asheville, but he never got interested in racing itself. As I said before, he was not interested in sports of any kind. Someone reading this may have heard of Fireball Roberts and Junior Johnson and other early drivers of that era.

He did like motors and things mechanical. He loved taking a motor apart and rebuilding it. He taught me how to do it and about what makes an engine work. He taught me how to grind out the cylinders using a special lathe, how to use a tool called a micrometer to measure the diameter of the cylinder to 1/1000th of an inch, and to grind and measure in that tiny dimension, and most important, why that makes the engine like new again and how and why cylinders of slightly different diameter changes a car's performance, plus all the other things that have to change when you make that tiny change in diameter. Today's engines are all digitized and so much more sophisticated that all of that knowledge is no longer applicable for today's mechanics, but show me an old '50s or '60s car, and I could still take it apart with the right tools. In those days I even liked getting my hands dirty.

Morty's Car The Mile Straight

We lived in the days of the one-car family. When Morty, the oldest, got his driver's license, he started lobbying for a car so he could go out with his friends, but all he could get was the use of the old, black, dirty, greasy 1954 International Harvester pick-up truck that was used at the store for just about everything. I believe he occasionally had a date, and an old dirty truck was hardly an attractive vehicle to take a girl in, let alone his other friends. I don't know if he could have used the family car or if he chose not to. After all, what 16-year-old boy wanted to be seen driving around in a huge 1954 Cadillac Fleetwood Sedan?

Have you ever seen one of those things? Even for those times it was huge and ostentatious. That's another thing. Why did Dad drive such a grand car in such a small, poor town? Mort and I have often wondered about that. He traded cars every couple of years, as I have mentioned, and some years he got a Pontiac or a Buick, but always went back to a Cadillac. Once, he brought home a little Plymouth. That one lasted about a six months, or maybe only three. That car definitely did not live up to family standards.

So Morty complained, but on Saturday afternoons, he would clean up that old truck as best he could and take off to wherever he went on

Saturday nights, and he lived with the situation. A second car was never in the budget, until…

As I've told you, Uncle Morris in Hendersonville was part of Louis Williams and Sons, which was a junk yard, hardware store, plumbing supply store, auto parts store, used-everything store, and a great place for little boys to play and get in trouble, fall down, and get hurt. But, as the little boys got older we began to notice that the junk yard part consisted of old cars, so Morty and I began to suggest to Uncle Morris that maybe one day he might haul in an old junk car that wasn't totally junk, that might have some use left in it. Well, Dad heard one of these conversations and, of course, killed the idea and said, "No way. Don't even think about it."

Uncle Morris and Dad were great friends, and it is my understanding that growing up being only two years apart, they were as close as brothers could be. Morris had a better sense of humor than Dad as I recall, and I believe he liked to be something of a prankster and "pull Dad's chain" once in a while. In any case, one day he announced—I don't remember if he told us (me and Morty) first or asked Dad first—that he had a car that might be salvageable. And the word got out that if we would send a wrecker he would give it to us. The condition that was agreed to was that we would rebuild and restore the car and make it usable. This must have been sometime in the late winter or early spring of Morty's junior year in high school, which would have been 1956 or so as he graduated high school in June of 1958.

And so the deal was struck that the car, a 1947 Chevrolet two-door sedan, six cylinder, was hauled to our garage in Canton, and Morty and I had a summer-long project of tearing that car apart from bumper to bumper and rebuilding it. I don't mind saying that I did most of the work because Morty *never* got his hands dirty or was anywhere around when work was being done.

We pulled the engine, the transmission, the front end, the rear end, the wheels, the brakes, steering; every part of that car was disassembled and reassembled. The interior wasn't in bad condition. I remember tearing out the head liner, the upholstered material in the ceiling of the car that covers up the all the wires and insulation separating the metal of the inside of the roof from the passengers, as it was pretty much rotted out, but the seats were okay. Since we had a glass cutting shop, we made new windshields and side glass where it was needed. This was before the days of curved windshields.

We didn't have a paint and body shop, and I don't remember if it needed body work, but I don't recall the body being in bad shape. I certainly don't remember spending any money on it for things that we couldn't do ourselves. But, of course, all the parts we used had to be paid for somehow. I suppose Dad bought them through his usual wholesale sources and never charged us for them. That was probably one of things it had going for it; that we didn't have to pay anyone to do anything we couldn't do ourselves. I'm sure the mechanics helped out a fair amount for the really technical stuff that we couldn't, or shouldn't, do.

When school started that fall, Morty had his car and he drove it his senior year of high school. Sadly, I never got to use it because it came to an unfortunate demise. Morty went off to college before I got my driver's license, so the car sat in the back of the garage unused, and we all know that it's not good for cars to sit unused; they have to be taken out and driven once in a while. So one day, Dad decided that we better take Mort's car out for a drive and rev it up to be sure everything's working okay. We got in the car and drove it down Canton Hill and Dad decided to take it out to the Mile Straight (remember…) to see how she'll do.

Those old cars with their three speed transmissions didn't have tachometers to tell you the engine speed and when to shift gears, when the engine was revving too fast, you had to do it by feel, by the sound of the engine, by experience. Dad starts at the top of the Mile Straight in first gear—just because I don't have my license yet doesn't mean I don't know how to drive, haven't been driving, don't know what an engine sounds like, and don't know when and how to shift gears. I'd been doing it since I was 12 or 13—and he winds the engine. "Daaad!" He shifts into second and winds the engine till it was screaming bloody murder! Dad's face is concentrating on the road, I'm looking at him, thinking, "What are you doing? Shift already!" His hands are gripping the wheel. How fast are we going? Glance at the speedometer (don't recall), feeling that this isn't going to end well. Grab the arm rest, push my feet against the floor boards, nothing to hold onto, want to push the brakes. Funny look on Dad's face as I look over. Does he really want to kill the car?

Then, Suddenly, "BLAAAMM!!!! sputtterrr sputtterrrr. "Daaaaad!" And I knew it was all over. All that work and now I was going have to try to do it all over but Mort was away at college. Was Dad going to let me rebuild the engine again? Oh well, my dream of my own car was probably gone.

Did you ever hear the sound of a connecting rod thrown through the side of an engine when you wind the engine too high and don't to shift to the next gear because you want to see how high the engine will rev? Trust me. You don't want to.

And that was the end of Mort's car on the infamous Mile Straight.

How did we get home? Was one of the mechanics following us? Was there someone on the road who saw what happened and picked us up? I have no memory. All I recall is wanting to rebuild the engine again and being told that you can't rebuild a thrown rod because, as I later saw, the rod literally went through the side of the engine block and Dad wouldn't let me buy a whole new engine block. So, back to uncle Morris's junk yard went the Chevy. End of story.

P.S. When Mort came home from college (UNC) and heard what happened to his car he was seriously, uh, unhappy.

Mom, Dad & the Buick on Academy St.
Canton, NC 1951

Morty and Joe
Miami circa 1952

Asheville

---◆---

In 1957, however the decision was finally arrived at, however many sleepless nights agonizing over that fateful decision before, during, and after the family meeting, it was decided to move to Asheville and stay in North Carolina.

My, how we were moving up in the world, and how much fun we had on the few days in the summer that it was actually warm enough to use the swimming pool at the house we bought at 8 Alclare Drive. And even fewer were the days we could get the filter system to work well enough to get the water clean enough to want to swim in it. The house is still there, a one-story, red-brick ranch house on the corner with a two car garage underneath in the full basement. The way the lot slopes and the way the house is built on the corner, the basement could actually accommodate four cars, two on each side if you pulled them all the way in and parked one behind the other. However, in typical Kaplan fashion, the first thing Dad did was a remodeling job. We closed up one side of the garage and made a really nice den downstairs and still had a two car garage on the other side, with one car behind the other. Then, at the far end of the basement he built a large room that eventually became my bedroom/ private hideaway when I was a senior in high school and during my first year of junior college.

The main part of the house was a very nice, three-bedroom, two-bathroom house with a large living room, dining room, kitchen, dinette, and small porch off the dining room where I liked to sit and watch the thunderstorms come in over Reynolds Mountain. I always loved sitting outside and watching thunderstorms. Years later, when Sue and I moved to Clearwater, Florida, we lived for a short time on Sand Key in a condo where we could watch the greatest thunderstorms in the world come in over the Gulf of Mexico and blow across Pinellas County and into Tampa Bay.

Alclare Drive was the nicest house we lived in all the years we lived in North Carolina and the one which holds some of the best memories, maybe because I was older—high school and all that. We had Jewish neighbors and my friend, David, lived around the corner. David and I learned to play golf together, double dated, and generally did a lot of early teenage stuff together. I was a year older so I had a driver's license first and had the use of a car. His mother was a single mom and appreciated his having someone in the neighborhood he could depend on to help out.

The street name, should you wonder, was a combination of the first names of the man and wife who developed the little subdivision; Al and Clare. I've forgotten their last names, Goodman seems to come to mind, but they built good houses, as the neighborhood still looks good and is a desirable location all these years later. It is located off Merrimon Avenue at the far end of Beaverdam Lake, if you happen to know your way around Asheville.

Since I just mentioned learning to play golf with my friend David, I'll tell you that story here as it's worth a mention, and I've been playing golf pretty much all of my life ever since, although you'd think I'd be a better golfer after all these years. But, like my basketball career, I'm not much of an athlete no matter the sport, I just like to go out and have a good time. Here's how my enjoyment for golf began:

My dad was even less of an athlete than me; he had no interest whatsoever in any sports at all, but he had a friend who played golf and was after him to learn to play. He kept nagging Dad and at some point Dad suggested that he teach me to play. I thought that was a great idea and asked if he would mind me bringing my friend David along, which of course was okay. I remember his friend as a man older than Dad, but I was only 14 or 15, so who knows, but I think he was 60ish at the time, not that it really matters to the story—I do wish I could remember his name.

Golf was beginning to become popular at this time, 1957-'58 the era of Slammin' Sammy Snead, Ben Hogan, and a young hot shot by the name of Arnold Palmer just coming up. There was a public golf course within walking distance of our home that we passed anytime we went to town, and there were private country clubs at the Grove Park Inn, The Asheville Country Club, and Biltmore, but we would never be allowed anywhere near those for a couple of reasons. First, they were private country clubs and secondly, even if someone would invite us, we would still not be allowed because there were restrictions in those against Jews, blacks, and others, but we could see them from the street occasionally. So we were lucky to have a public course so near to home. As young teenagers, golf was a sport we wanted to learn to play if only because it was so inaccessible and looked so exotic; so when the opportunity came, we jumped at it.

The first thing our new friend did was take us to his house to get us some golf clubs. I will never forget going into his garage and seeing the walls lined with shelves full of golf clubs! He was a collector of golf clubs, he told us, and he would outfit us with a few old clubs each to get us started. Well, if you know anything about the history of golf clubs, and you remember this was 1957 or thereabouts, you can imagine the golf clubs we started out with. I recall a couple of hickory-shafted beauties with names like—Names? Oh yes, there were no numbers in those days—the clubs were called mashies, niblick, niblick-mashie, a driver, a woodie, a putter, a wedge; David and I had maybe five or six all together and a beat-up old canvas bag to carry them in. Then there was this huge bin full of balls, if you want to call them that. Did you ever see a featherie? It was an old ball stuffed with feathers. A true collector's item, even then. He picked through the bin and found a bunch of the least bad ones, the ones that were reasonably round, without too many cuts and dings. He added some tees to our outfit and pronounced us ready to take our first lesson.

The only thing is, our first lesson had nothing to do with golf clubs or golf balls or golf courses or golf swings or any of those things. It was about behavior, etiquette, and the game of golf. He taught us golf history, how to play the game, and the rules and why they were important. He talked about golf and life and how the two go together, how you can tell a lot about a person by the way they behave on a golf course. Golf is a game of honor. There are no referees. No one is calling balls and strikes, throwing flags, calling fouls. You hit the ball and play it where it lies. If you move it, only you know. Do you trust your opponent to play honestly? It's between you and him and God. If you're honest on the golf course, you'll be honest in life, in business. Here's this old man talking to two kids. I never forgot his words of wisdom. By the way, he was right.

I've never forgotten that introduction to golf and think about it when I'm on the golf course with people I don't know. I watch their behavior and realize that they never had that lesson, that they know nothing about golf, about how to behave on the golf course; that there are rules, that there is etiquette, and a history; that golf is more than seeing how hard you can swing the club and how badly you can dress.

Then he said if we were still interested we could come back and he would start by showing us how to hold a golf club and begin learning how to swing. He let us know that there was a lot more to golf then we thought. We agreed to a date and time, and so began my lifelong attempt to learn to play golf.

If you've never seen a mashie, let me try to describe what it looked like. The shaft was made of hickory wood. Hickory was used because it is incredibly strong yet flexible, doesn't rot, and is impervious to things like termites. In fact, when I go into an old houses, down in the basement or crawl space, I sometimes will find old hickory posts still holding up the house, driven into the ground decades ago, hard as steel, and looking perfectly fine.

The grip of the club was a length of leather about one-inch wide wrapped around the shaft and glued on. When it came loose, the 1950 version of duct tape was added to hold it in place.

The actual club face was a thin piece of solid forged steel with grooves incised in it. It felt like it weighed a ton—how anyone actually played the kind of championship golf they played in those days with those clubs remains a mystery to me. After a few lessons I was able to actually hit the ball and get it airborne with those clubs, after all, that's all I knew; those were my golf clubs. But, having learned to play with them and then over the years graduating to modern technology as it progressed certainly made me appreciate what we have today.

The most amazing thing about the gentleman who taught us was the level of skill he possessed. He had been playing all of his life and now played with only one club, which in today's parlance, would be considered about a 4.5 iron. He could consistently shoot in the mid-80s; he had total control of that ball.

The golf course where David and I learned to play is now the Asheville Country Club; in those days it was a public course and they would let us on in the evenings for a dollar or two. We would go out after dinner and play until it was too dark to see, playing multiple balls when no one else was around, practicing until we got to be pretty good. Then we'd walk home.

The gas station

Dad decided to buy a gas station. It was called Newbridge Shell, and I became intimately familiar with its operation over the couple of years that we owned it. I don't know exactly why he decided to buy it, other than the desire to have another auto-related business near to our new home in Asheville. After we moved to Asheville, we still owned and operated Kay's Auto Parts in Canton. Mort completed his senior year at Canton High and I did my sophomore year and played basketball there, as I said earlier. At some point in that year, Dad bought the gas station, and I had a new job. I learned how to run a full-service gas station. I learned how to pump gas when pumping gas involved actually doing work to make the pump work. You had to turn a crank on the side of the pump to reset the counter and turn it on and hold the hose in place to keep the fuel flowing. You would talk to the customer, check the oil and the water, sell a quart of oil, fill the radiator, check the tires, wash the windshield—anybody remember those days? All for 18¢ a gallon, maybe it was 26¢ by then. Those services defined the full-service gas station. That means I did everything. I changed oil, lubed cars, fixed flats, rotated tires, sold batteries, washed cars, waxed cars, replaced spark plugs, etc. We had a tow truck, and I didn't have a license to drive it, but that didn't stop me from driving it around the parking lot and learning how to drive it, work the mechanism, etc. And it was almost entirely a cash business as this pre-dates credit cards; the only non-cash business were regular customers who had credit accounts or whose checks we'd take with confidence.

For two summers I worked full time, meaning 50- or 60-hour weeks. Remember my talk of coming home dirty as a little boy? Now I came home dirty, greasy, and exhausted. I don't think the business ever made any money because the margins on gasoline were so slight that you were always practically giving it away. So, mercifully, Dad finally gave up and sold it, probably because I was going off to college and there was no way to hire anyone you could trust. As it was, theft was also a big problem. I learned a lot of lessons about running small, cash businesses. The main one being, the only way to run one is to do it all yourself or they don't work.

Asheville Battery Company

Kay's Auto Parts was finally shut down. I don't know the details; I never thought about it until now, I wish I did. What did my parents do with the inventory? Moved it to Asheville Battery Company probably, that would be the logical thing. But what about the actual decision? How did they decide what day to close? Did they have a sale? An announcement? Did they just close the door and drive away? What were their emotions? I have no idea. I don't remember my parents as being outwardly emotional people, or people who cried or yelled; they certainly never fought. What did they feel after leaving behind 11 years of hard work? Relief?

In Leonard Rogoff's book, Down Home, Jewish Life in North Carolina, his history of the Jews of North Carolina, he describes how the Jewish merchants had a long history of coming into a town, establishing themselves for a few years, and then moving on when their business didn't prosper as expected in that town. My parent's experience in Canton certainly fits that pattern to a T.

However it was arrived at, the decision was made and the page was turned. Asheville Battery Company on Coxe Avenue in Asheville was purchased. Asheville Battery Company was a well-established business with two specialty niches in the automotive market place. Unfortunately, neither was to last long.

Early on in the book I spoke of my family's journey as a micro example of the larger economic forces that drive decision-making and that drive our fates. I believe those forces can very much be seen in this next story.

All roads lead to the competition

With the end of the Korean War, the American economy entered into an unprecedented boom, the likes of which had never before been seen. President Eisenhower began the largest highway development program in history—the interstate highway program—cars were pouring out of Detroit, Michigan. The United States was the world leader in almost every field of industry. The American consumer had money and the market was providing goods for him to buy. This boom penetrated even to the small mountain communities of Canton and Asheville and the rest of Western North Carolina. As a result, the small independent retailers such as Kay's Auto Parts and Asheville Battery Co. could no longer maintain their profit margins; they just weren't needed any longer because the manufacturers would rather sell to larger retailers who would sell directly to consumers at prices lower than we could buy items for, thus putting us out of business. Our customers in Canton could easily drive to Asheville now, to the big modern stores and have a better selection in nicer stores and pay less.

Dad bought a business about to be put out of business and had no way of seeing it coming. Asheville Battery Company was the exclusive distributor for Prestone Antifreeze, the biggest name for antifreeze in the country at the time, for all of Western North Carolina, eastern Tennessee, parts of southern Virginia and northwestern Georgia—a huge territory worth hundreds or thousands of dollars a year in business at the time. In addition, it had a similar distributorship for Williard Batteries, which was the authorized replacement battery for all General Motors cars. So all GM dealers bought batteries from us, and independent garages who wanted a factory-authorized replacement battery for their customer had to buy from us, exclusively. Thus the name Asheville BATTERY Company. We sold a wide variety of other kinds of auto parts as well, but batteries were the bread-and-butter of the business—why it had value—and why Dad bought it.

The business also had its own repair shop that did specialty auto repairs. We worked only on the electrical and fuel systems and we repaired batteries. We actually had a shop that took batteries apart and rebuilt them and sold them as used, rebuilt batteries.

I don't remember exactly how long after we bought it that the bad news came; whether it was right away or a year or two. I think it was later rather than sooner. And I wonder, of course if the seller knew what was coming. Dad would never do such a thing, but today you know the lawyers would be sharpening their pencils over who knew what and when and just what those contracts looked like.

A day came when Prestone informed us that they were canceling their arrangement, whatever it was—a franchise or a distributorship, I don't know. Prestone said they would be selling their antifreeze to all retailers, and we soon saw it up the street in the Sears store. Sears would mark it down as a loss leader to less than our cost, and that killed a big chunk of our business.

Williard Batteries soon followed suit, although in not so drastic a way. They severely cut back on our exclusive territory, but also allowed us to carry competing brands, which we did and we always maintained a substantial battery business, but at much lower margins.

The loss of the antifreeze business was devastating and really destroyed the economic basis of the business and the reason for buying it. Perhaps a more astute business man/analyst than my father would have seen that coming and not bought it, would have seen the broader, macro-economic picture, but I kind of doubt it. I don't know that anyone in a place like Asheville in 1957 thought like that.

What happened to Asheville Battery Company? What did it become? Ultimately, like Kay's Auto Parts, Asheville Battery Company closed its doors. I tried to keep it going through the winter of 1963 but was too young and inexperienced and had my Army enlistment coming up in February of 1964. The cash flow—I didn't even know that phrase then—gradually deteriorated until there was nothing left, and sometime early in 1964, Dad locked the doors and walked away. Once again, he never told me the gory details of how much money he lost or how the pieces were sold and I didn't know what questions to ask. It faded away into family history never to be spoken of.

In 1957, when you drove into Asheville from the west, up Patton Avenue and turned right down Coxe Avenue, the thing that would strike you was that this was automobile row. All the way down the hill were auto dealers, used car lots, and auto parts stores; right and left, that's about all you'd see. Chevrolet, Buick, Pontiac, Hudson, Packard, (Hudson?, Packard? What's he talking about? I'll leave it to you and Google) Ford, and about two-thirds of the way on the right was the white building that said Asheville Battery Company. There were three garage doors to pull into for service or you could park by the front door or pull into the side alley and drive around back and park.

Cars and characters

If you came in the front door you'd immediately be greeted by the parts counter with its ubiquitous parts books and at least one salesman working the counter to help you. Usually it would be "Brownie," with the bad front teeth and the pipe hanging out of his mouth. Behind the counter you'd see four rows of auto parts and to the right the small office. Poke your head in the office—there's no door—and you'd see Mom sitting at her desk and to her left the bookkeeper, Noble Childers from Pikeville, Kentucky, and he would always have stories to tell, sitting behind his big posting machine. That was a semi-automatic bookkeeping machine which was an early attempt at automating the bookkeeping process, not worth a lot of explanation but he loved pushing all the buttons instead having to enter everything the old fashioned way by hand in big ledgers. It was a big improvement in efficiency. If he was sober.

Walk down the hallway between the office and the last row of parts, and you'd come to a door to the garage on your right or a door straight ahead to the back warehouse full of batteries, and during the season, Prestone Antifreeze, tire chains, and all the other merchandise that needed a place to be stored.

The repair garage had three bays where cars could pull in; I think three or four cars at most could be crowded in. Two were reserved primarily for general car repairs and the third was usually used for the battery shop but could be used for anything as the need arose. We were still in the day of repairing things instead of throwing them away and replacing everything with new, although that day could be seen on the horizon as a threat to our business as replacement parts got cheaper and labor more expensive.

We had one old mechanic, Mickey (funny how his name came to me as I was writing this), a small, wizened old man with a cigarette always hanging out of his mouth, needing a shave. He was an expert at repairing carburetors, generators, and starters; that's all he'd work on. If you're too young to know what those are—or were, as modern cars don't have them—then I suggest you Google them. Try searching on 1958 Pontiac Bonneville with double four barrels and learn something about the history of the internal combustion engine as it is too complicated to go into here. Suffice it to say that a carburetor, by the mid-50s was an immensely complicated bit of engineering with hundreds of tiny parts that had to work together in absolute harmony for the car's engine to hum along in smooth perfection, which it seldom did.

In the years 1955 to the early '60s the auto manufactures started playing with adding multiple carburetors to big V-8 engines creating monsters like triple two barrels and dual four barrels. Oh, they were such heaven to hear when they worked perfectly, the sounds they made, especially when "souped up" and added glass pack mufflers to make them really roar!

Ah, but I'm getting carried away with my teenage nostalgia. Back to Mickey. Mickey's job was to make all these parts actually work together, consistently, and even without all the add-ons and hot rods, it was a hard enough job because the engineering was great on the drawing board but all these intricate little parts wore out. Mickey was a master at taking the things apart and putting them back together again. He could listen to a car's engine and diagnose what was wrong and what needed to be replaced. I can remember him telling me, "Get in the car, start the engine, give her a little gas," and I'd watch him listen; turn his head just so. "Ease off now, he'd say." Then, "race it a little more. Okay. Turn it off." He had his diagnosis, just like a doctor. He knew what needed to be fixed. Sometimes he'd turn those little adjusting screws on the carburetor that controlled the mixture and ratio of gas to air that entered the cylinders and you'd and feel the engine change and sometimes only he'd hear it until he got it running just right. There are and were tools and gauges that helped judge those things but he did it by feel in those days.

We had a whole floor-to-ceiling set of shelves full of tiny, indescribable little pieces for the carburetors for every American car made from the 1930s to the 1960s. I can no longer begin to name them, but in my teen years I knew just what they were.

Mickey himself was a piece of work. You couldn't hurry him or speak harshly to him as he knew he had a great skill and was in demand. He was a prima donna in his field and commanded respect in the auto mechanic's world of Asheville of the 1950s. He taught me a lot about how cars worked.

We had a couple of other interesting characters working for us, but the one I tell people about that no one believes was old Zeb. Now Zeb was an old-timey country character who lived way, way out in the mountains. Zeb rolled his own cigarettes and tried to teach me how to do it, but I never quite caught on. Zeb told me one time how he got to work every day. He said the he drove his old pick-up truck about 20 miles up the mountain, and then when he couldn't get any further, he parked it and took the old Model T Ford he'd had since he was a young'un, but it would only go so far, so then he'd have to git out and walk the last mile or so. This was to tell me about his young granddaughter. "You see," he said, "I have this young granddaughter who has the purtiest, gol dang singin' voice anyone in those parts ever did hear in church ever Sundee." Now Zeb told me this through a haze of cigarette smoke and, oh, I forgot to tell you, Zeb's last name was Parton and his granddaughter's first name was Dolly! Yes, that Dolly who you may have heard of. The little girl with the "Purtiest gol darn voice anybody in them parts any body ever did hear of."

Zeb's job was to do whatever needed to be done and he was a good man. He learned how to repair batteries, to take them apart by melting the tar on top, draining the sulphuric acid out, taking out the lead plates, and replacing them, then putting the whole works back together and replacing the lead terminals on top. Nice work, huh? Working with lead, sulphuric acid, and hot tar. But that was the world in those days—fix it, don't throw it away. Today we don't fix anything, everything is disposable. You decide which is better.

After losing the two big money-makers Asheville Battery Company survived—barely—and Dad and Mom eked out a living for the next couple of years. I don't know what the numbers were and I wasn't really conscious of the level of profitability or lack thereof, but I could feel that things weren't going particularly well. Just being in the store every day as I was, I could sense the level of sales wasn't good, the phone wasn't ringing enough, there weren't enough sales tickets in the drawer at the end of every day.

We had two or three outside salesmen traveling the outlying counties calling on various kinds of garages and mechanics, and they brought in business, but I know they stole a great deal of merchandise and it was difficult to put a stop to it. Dad would catch them and they'd pay him back and swear to stop, but he wasn't tough enough; he was afraid of them, I could sense it.

They were all also drunks. Brownie on the front counter and two or three salesmen would always come in after lunch smelling of liquor. I recognized this after I got old enough to realize what the smell was and how their demeanor changed. I began to recognize the change in behavior too, and it scared me, and I swore that I would never, ever employ a drunk no matter what the consequence. Dad would never fire these men because he felt that he needed the business they brought in; he worried that if he fired them, they would take business to a competitor, and he couldn't afford that. At a young age I felt he was wrong, that they were stealing more than they could possibly be worth, that we should find new people and train them and send them out to compete for the business. But these were only instincts of a young kid that I had no way to put into practice. I'm still sure I was right, but he had his own reasons and wouldn't take the risks. In my business life I've never been able to work around anyone I've suspected of drinking on the job. I can't stand that strange, unfocused look, slurred speech, knowing you can't trust anything they do or say. Which isn't to say I have anything against drinking at the appropriate time and place, just not at work.

Dad's other major problem that, to this day, I cannot understand was his absolute refusal to advertise and to market himself. He never ever paid for a single advertisement of any kind with any media. I can remember all kinds of meetings, discussions, arguments with friends in other kinds of retail as well as advertising and marketing salespeople trying to convince him of the efficacy and advantages of getting his name out if front of the public. But he had this strange notion that the community knew we were there, and if they needed our service they would find us. I even tried arguing with him in my own naïve way, but what did I know, what experience did I have? He could never be convinced. I believe to this day that with an aggressive marketing program, the business could have been turned into something successful in the Asheville automobile marketplace as it had an old and trusted name and presence in Asheville. Even after all the auto-related businesses moved off of Coxe Avenue, it could have moved with them. But Lou Kaplan was a scholar and teacher and not a businessman and marketer and so he didn't do what needed to be done.

Being Jewish in Asheville

Altogether I lived in Asheville about five years, including the year of commuting back to Canton to finish the 10th grade and the first year of college at Asheville-Biltmore College. But that is somewhat misleading because the entire time we lived in Canton, we had been commuting to Asheville for our religious life and a good portion of our social life, so finally living there was not as wrenching a change as it might otherwise have been. I knew all of the Jewish kids in and around Asheville, particularly the ones whose families were members of the Conservative Synagogue, now known and Beth Israel but in the early years had the name Bikur Cholim which is literally translated as "visiting the sick" which is one of the 613 commandments. Why it was chosen as the name for a synagogue back in, I believe 1898, I have no idea. The name was changed sometime in the 1960's.

For those of you may not be familiar with Jewish internal divisions and politics, a brief digression is in order. By the 1950s, there were three major strains of Judaism in America: The old, original Orthodoxy maintained the most fundamental beliefs, to use a modern, though imperfect, analogy. In the early 19th century, in Germany, it was beginning to be modified, and when it was brought to these shores, it became known as Reform Judaism. It was a radical reaction to Orthodox belief and practice.

In reaction to the radical change of Reform, a typical American response grew up that tried to bridge the gap between the two, and this became known as Conservatism. It was for those who didn't want to reject all of the old practices but also didn't want to go as far as Reform. So most towns and cities with Jewish communities ended up having at least two distinct Jewish communities: one Reform Temple, and, usually smaller, Conservative Synagogue, and perhaps an old, much smaller Orthodox Synagogue, barely hanging on and fading rapidly.

Asheville was such a community where the orthodox remnant had faded into the Conservative Synagogue and that is where my family belonged. The Reform was typically made up of descendants of the older German immigrant families who had come to America much earlier in the nineteenth century and were wealthier, whereas the Conservative families were more recent immigrant families of Russian and other Eastern European descent, frequently first-generation immigrants. There was a distinct class differentiation and discrimination within the Jewish communities in Asheville as well as most other communities.

I know, I know, this brief overview is an oversimplification and leaves out a lot but it is not meant to be a history of the Jewish People so please hold your criticism.

There were about 60 or 70 families, maybe 100, who were members of the Conservative Synagogue and I knew all of them as we were regular members. We attended services regularly, driving to Asheville most Friday nights and attending all the holiday services. My paternal grandparents moved to Asheville about 1948 or '49, so this is a good place to talk about them, as their living in Asheville had an effect on my life in Asheville as well. However, to tell that story, I have to back up all the way back to the beginning of this narrative.

It would be interesting to know what went on back there in 1946 when Uncle Morris married Ann and moved to Hendersonville, then Mom and Dad left Scranton and followed them to nearby Canton. Grampa sold the farm in Pennsylvania sometime around the end of the war, and I think there was a big fight about that, which may have been part of the reason Dad left—over money, of course. I think Uncle Bernie and Uncle Seymour went to Philadelphia. Seymour had a degree in fine arts from the Philadelphia College of Art, which he had completed before the war, and he wanted to try to do something with that. He got into advertising, which he did for some time, as well as illustrating. We have a couple of books he illustrated and he was very talented. Bernie somehow bought a couple of row houses on Pine Street and Spruce Street that he remodeled and rented. Mort and I think they did it together: Bernie, Seymour, and Grampa. Then in 1948 or 1949, Uncle Bernie and my grandparents came to Asheville and bought a house on Austin Avenue, and Seymour stayed in Philadelphia alone; I think he was employed in advertising or public relations, illustrating or doing something utilizing his art, and within a year or so met his wife, Shirley. Wouldn't it have been nice to have been the proverbial fly on the wall to understand the motivations that sent the whole family following Uncle Morris to North Carolina? No one will ever know.

Back to my Asheville story

Back to my story. Now we're all in Asheville and you know how we got here. In the Canton years we'd come to Asheville on Friday nights, often early enough to have Shabbos (Sabbath) dinner at Grandma's and then walk to shul (synagogue) if it was a nice summer evening, or more likely pile into the car and drive the few blocks. Oh, by the way, remember it was the Kaplans who bought the house on Austin Avenue, so guess what, the first thing they did to the house was to tear it apart and remodel it. Uncle Bernie decided that they could divide it down the middle, make a duplex out of it, and rent one half. So for the next—who knows, a year?—they all lived in the middle of one of Uncle Bernie's construction projects and eventually they had a tenant. When I moved back to Hendersonville a few years ago, I went looking for the house and someone over the years put it back the way it was, because it no longer appears to be a duplex.

When Morty and I got a little older, 9 or 10 or thereabouts, we went to Asheville for Friday nights and then we would stay overnight with Grandma and Grampa and go to Saturday service with Grampa and Uncle Bernie. In the Jewish tradition, the Saturday service is the important one as the Sabbath day is actually Saturday. One of the major changes that Reform Judaism made was to drop the Saturday service altogether, which was likely one of the driving factors in our attending the Conservative Synagogue. We would spend the weekend in Asheville, sometimes spending Saturday night as well if there was something going on at the Jewish Community Center on Sunday that we wanted to attend. Mom and Dad would drive to Asheville on Sunday to spend the day and bring us home. Other times we would take the bus back to Canton on Saturday afternoon. Looking back, I realize that those were wonderful weekends spent with my grandparents. My grandfather died in 1955 at age 72, of what today would have been a mild, almost routine heart attack, but at that time there was no cardiac care available in Asheville, and there was nothing they could do to save him. My grandmother lived on to what is believed to be about 90 or 92—she never really knew her birth date. We have pictures of her holding my children, her great grandchildren.

I remember walking into her house and smelling her wonderful cooking—I can still almost taste that delicious homemade food. The chicken soup, the stuffed cabbage, the challah, the noodles she made; she made everything from scratch, no recipes, nothing was ever written down. She was an artist with bread dough. When she baked she would shape the dough into our initials or into farm animals, she created all kinds of treats for us. They were wonderful foods that were full of ingredients that we would consider artery-clogging anathema today, ingredients such as chicken fat (schmaltz), all kinds of organ meats, etc. Ah, but I loved going there and eating. "Ess yuselleh, ess" I can still hear her saying, which, in English means, "Eat, Joey, eat."

Both my parents spoke Yiddish before they spoke English. Though he was born here, Dad always said he only learned English at about age five when he went to kindergarten. His parents came here as immigrants from Russia, and Yiddish was the only language they spoke at home. I once asked my grandmother about Russian, whether she knew how to speak it, and she reluctantly admitted knowing some Russian but said she refused to ever speak it. However, as was typical for their generation, they didn't want their children to know Yiddish. This was partly so they would have a "secret" language, so they could talk without us understanding, but more because they wanted their children to be one hundred percent American—it was something of a shame factor, I believe. It's sad that today's immigrants don't feel the same way about this country.

Whatever their motivation, I've been mad at them over that decision all my life. The opportunity to speak a second language from birth is such a loss to me; any second language. During those weekends in Asheville, Grandma used to try to teach us a little Yiddish, most of which I've forgotten, but a few phrases stuck with me. I remember her drilling us on proper words whenever we'd sit down to eat. She'd have us repeat the words for all the kitchen utensils for instance, knife, fork, spoon, plate, etc. Don't ask, I've forgotten them all. Once, she taught us what I thought was a nursery rhyme—she had a wicked sense of humor—and told me not tell my mother when I got home. So I memorized the few lines of Yiddish, and dutifully went on to share it with Mom. Mom asked if Grandma told me what I was saying. Needless to say, she was not pleased. It was not nice and I won't repeat it here. That bit of Yiddish, of course, I still remember. But I'm afraid that it was something so not nice that it would offend some people so I am not going to say. Let's just say that the Jews of eastern Europe were generally badly treated and discriminated against, so they made up songs and rhymes that were insulting to their tormentors.

The house on Austin Avenue had a large porch all the way across the front. In the summer we used to sit out there in the evenings and pass the time together. There were other Jewish families on the street, next door, across the street; the Schandlers were a couple of houses down. After services on warm Friday nights, people would gather on our porch for coffee and visit for a while; on Sunday afternoons there would be people dropping by on and off. It was a totally different atmosphere and experience than living in Canton (a neighborhood in which we'd keep pretty much to ourselves). It was two entirely different worlds that we were living among. Kind of strange, but lovely if you think about it.

When I wrote earlier about never being part of the social fabric of Canton, you can see that we really did separate ourselves from Canton. We lived in Canton during the week, went to school there, but come the weekend, we were in Asheville most of the time, which was the real focus of our social life. Between the ages of 10 and 11 years old when I started preparing for bar mitzvah and going to Saturday morning services almost every week, I was totally separate from any weekend activities in Canton. I was really in kind of an impossible situation. The kids I spent most of my time with all week, those I saw every day in school and would be expected to know the best, I would have almost no opportunity to be with on the weekends. I missed the opportunity to socialize with school friends at parties, to go out with them on Saturday night, etc. And those that I socialized with on the weekends, though I enjoyed them, I really didn't know all that well. It was tough because we lacked the common experiences of the same teachers, classes, and weekday activities in Canton. I never thought of any of that until I started writing this, but now, I believe I have some insight into why I never had close friends especially in the critical adolescent years. The kind of buddies you shared everything with. And, of course, why I never had girlfriends, never dated. In Canton not only was there the *not Jewish* problem, but I also wasn't there on the weekend. In Asheville, I only saw other children on the weekend during the couple of early years of junior high school and 9th and 10th grade when close friendships, cliques if you will, are formed. By the time I was going to school in Asheville in 11th grade, it was too late to break into that society. This is not to say that I didn't have friends and acquaintances but not the close friendships that last a lifetime.

Mort and I went to Shul on Saturday mornings, came home for lunch and sometimes walked to a friend's house and spent the afternoon doing whatever kids did. There was a group of boys and girls our age who were more or less regular attendees on Saturday as it was required to go to Saturday services a certain amount of time to be bar mitzvahed. It was part of the training.

There were about 10–15 kids, a few of them within five years of my age older or younger. If my grandparents moved to Asheville in 1948, and we moved to Asheville in 1957, then Mort and I probably spent at least part of every weekend there from 1952 or '53 until we moved, that is at least every Friday night. I don't recall objecting or rebelling at all. I kind of liked spending time with family, immersed in our cultural traditions, being with my grandfather, my uncle, going to services and being with the other Jewish boys. In my memory it is a very positive time.

The JCC (Jewish Community Center)

While our religious life in Asheville centered around the synagogue there was another institution in Asheville that played a large part and had a significant influence on my growing up. That was the JCC. Asheville has long been known as the smallest city in America to have a full-time functioning Jewish Community Center. I don't know when the JCC started, but it was there when we came to the area in the late 1940s.

As I have written, we usually came to Asheville on Friday nights for Shabat (Sabbath) services and would return home late at night. Later, after my grandparents moved to Asheville and Morty and I began preparation for our bar mitzvahs, we would spend Friday nights with our grandparents in order to go the Saturday services.

For the children whose families were members of our synagogue living in Asheville there was a weekday after-school Hebrew school which was held at the JCC, which we were not able to attend due the difficulty of traveling from Canton on a weekday afternoon. There was, however, an additional day of Sunday school which, now that our grandparents lived in Asheville, we began attending. So our weekends in Asheville became three-day affairs. Friday nights we drove in with our parents for a family dinner and services, Saturday services with grandparents, Uncle Bernie, many friends, Saturday night followed by Sunday school at the JCC, and then Mom and Dad would show up for Sunday afternoon gatherings on Austin Ave and eventually drive home. Sometimes Uncle Morris and family would drive in from Hendersonville.

My memories of the JCC are the memories of the main source of any formal Jewish education until my father took over teaching me one-on-one at the store, as I have described elsewhere.

I have one particularly strong memory of those early days of going to Sunday school. It occurred on or about May 14, 1948. I was a very little boy of about five and a half, and it's hard to believe the memory could be so strong, but if that date means anything to you, you know it was the date of the founding of the State of Israel. It must have been the Sunday right after the United Nations voted to declare Israel a state and I can distinctly recall standing in the big foyer of the old building (it was a big old house) and Dad and a group of other men were standing talking excitedly about this amazing event. "We have a state." Israel was approved. Truman got it done. I don't know if those were the words I heard, who could remember what a little boy heard so many years ago, but I know it was something like that and I can still feel the excitement they expressed that Israel had come into existence. Tears still come into my eyes when I recall looking up into their faces trying to comprehend what I was hearing. Later, I asked Dad what had happened and he explained that we Jews had our own country, as best he could to a five year old, but it made such an impression that I have never forgotten it, and every time I've gone there I remember that moment.

For the Asheville Jewish Community the JCC was a lot more than Beth Israel's Sunday school. The other Temple, Beth Ha-Tephila, had a building large enough to have its own school. It was a gathering place and a meeting place for a myriad of community events, parties, affairs, organizations, etc.

As far as I know it has always been located at 236 Charlotte St. The original building that I knew as a child was a big old white mansion on the left side of the street as you drive down Charlotte St. going out of town. Up a flight of steps from the street you'd go in the big front doors to the entrance hall. On the right was what must have originally been the library, but was used as the administrator's office. Down the hall to the back was the kitchen, and up the big staircase were the classrooms. On the left was the large room which was used as a meeting room and through the meeting room were stairs that led down to a ballroom with a stage where we had parties.

Ah, yes, parties. When I came of age, which I think was at thirteen, I joined AZA/BBYO, the Jewish youth organization which met at the JCC. The main purpose of this group was to have unmanageable meetings whose purpose was to plan the next party, meet girls, play ball, and have fun. This was my introduction to organizations/clubs; to committees and elections and politics. It was where I first learned that some people are organized and can run meetings and others can't and only create chaos. I also learned that over time, nothing changes, groups are the same whether the members are 16 or 60.

Now my weekends in Asheville expanded from just going to religious services and Sunday school (which ended after age thirteen) to AZA meetings and related events, committees, parties etc.

By the time we moved to Asheville the JCC built a swimming pool and became even more the center of our social life, especially in the summer time. Which brings me to one last story.

Across the street from the JCC are apartments which was once a resort hotel, sort of a less expensive Grove Park Inn. One sunny early summer Sunday afternoon between my junior and senior years in high school, a family from NYC consisting of a mother, father and cute teenage daughter showed up at the pool interested in meeting the local Jewish community as they were in town for the summer. The daughter was conveniently a year younger than me and I just happened to be there along with my friend David to greet her. It took about 30 seconds and he and I were falling all over each other to impress her. Need I paint the picture any more graphically? Two teenage boys who haven't seen a new face in town since forever, meeting an exotic, adorable, teenage girl from New York City of all places, actually looking to meet boys! Was this some kind of movie script? That night's date included her and the two of us.

After a whirlwind of small town dates, ideas, and promises, typical of teenagers, we parted ways at the end of the summer. Although we did keep in touch through our college years and saw each other from time to time eventually our friendship faded away to a pleasant memory of an unexpected summer romance.

And to think it all started at the JCC in Asheville. Eventually, I met the love of my life, Susan. Thank heavens it didn't work out with NYC girl.

Lee H Edwards High School

I don't know when they changed the name to Asheville High School; sometime after I graduated in 1960. I was told that Lee H Edwards, for whom the school was originally named, was an old-time segregationist governor or politician, and that obviously wouldn't be appropriate in the politically correct world that came into being after the schools were integrated. None of that was taught to us when we studied the history of North Carolina as we came up through the school system back in those innocent years.

I came into Lee Edwards as a junior and it was a major change from what I was used to in Canton. First of all, the school building was and still is a relatively huge, physically imposing, white stone building built in a "Y" shape with a central rotunda. To enter, you climb a long flight of stone steps up to the front door. As you pass through the front doors, you enter the main rotunda where there are long, wide hallways lined with lockers—at least there were in 1958, I have no idea what it looks like inside now as I haven't been inside since the day I graduated in June 1960. I remember being immediately overwhelmed and lost, but I soon got over it and found my way around as generations before and after me have done in every high school everywhere.

The questions of whether or not I should try out for the basketball team came up a couple of times, but I was advised by my buddies from AZA that I wouldn't have a chance. First of all, I hadn't come up through the Junior Varsity team, and Lee Edwards was in a much tougher conference than Canton as it was a larger school. The team was set and was expected to do well for the next couple of years, so I wouldn't have much of a chance given my basic skill level to begin with. I attended a couple of practices just to see for myself what was going on and decided that I had better things to do than beat myself up over something that probably wasn't going to happen. So that pretty much ended my high school bas- ketball career.

During my last two years in high school, I discovered that there were things I liked learning, but I had a great deal of difficulty being successful and making good grades. I just couldn't pass tests. I discovered I liked math and could do algebra, geometry, and trigonometry because they were logical and one step followed the next. In chemistry and physics, I struggled memorizing formulas but loved the theories about how things worked. And then I discovered history and political science and realized that I found where I wanted to be. I discovered what I really wanted to learn more about and those are the topics I have been reading and studying and arguing about ever since. I also learned that I could write well. I had good English teachers who taught us the basics of English grammar and sentence structure; I even remember learning to diagram sentences and actually liked it because, of course, you know, it's logical and I love things that are logical and make sense. It's so sad, such a loss, that our modern day education system has given up on all of the basics of spelling and grammar and sentence structure. I think that is why communication has become so bad between and among people today. If you can't form a simple sentence, how can you formulate a thought to create a logical argument? All people are able to do is yell and scream nonsense at each other so it seems.

Where was I? Oh yes, I had some good teachers who taught me to write and to read history and to make arguments. The problem was that I just couldn't pass the tests. Multiple choice became multiple guess questions; fill-in-the-blanks, true/false, these were my death knell. I could know the material backwards and forwards, but that instant recall at exam time simply wasn't there. So I was the kid in the back of the room who, on the first day of the semester, raised his hand and asked how many term papers we had to write, how many book reports could I do, and was there any other way to earn extra credit? Everyone would turn, staring daggers at me, hissing, "Shut UP!" But the only way I could pass most classes was to write papers, and so I did. I learned how to use the library and I loved doing research papers.

In order to write papers I had to know how to type because I also was blessed with the world's worst hand writing. Lee Edwards had a secretarial track for the girls, of course. Talking about being non-politically correct! Luckily, boys were allowed to take the courses, so a few of us signed up for beginning typing, and am I ever glad I took it. It was worth its weight in gold when I was a private in the Army and the call went out for someone who could type—but that's another story.

The course was taught using ancient Underwood and Royal upright typewriters that weighed in at 50 or 60 pounds each with the letter keys blanked out, meaning the keys didn't have the letter printer on them so you couldn't tell which letter you were typing. The text books were red books that opened from the top. The course was pure memorization and repetition, over and over. Put your four fingers on the middle keys: ASDF, thumbs on the space bar, JKL; and type them one at a time, saying the names over and over until they're stuck in your head for the rest of your life. After a couple of hours of that you never ever needed to see the letter printed on those keys again. Then you'd add one letter at a time to the repetition, adding letters until those were stuck in your brain as well. And it worked for millions of high school kids for generations. Who knows how many of us learned to type this way in a very short period of time; I've never forgotten and have been using it all my life ever since.

The first semester of typing was easy. You could make an A in class by being able to type 30 or 40 words per minute with 80 or 90% accuracy. Pretty much anybody could do that. The second semester got boring. This was, after all, a secretarial course and we boys had no interest in being secretaries, but we were committed to both semesters. The second semester was all about learning the proper way to write letters, correspondence, letter heads, invoices, envelopes, etc. I had less and less interest as the semester wore on. And you know what happens to grades as interest turns to boredom. So an easy A in the first semester gradually deteriorated to, well, let's say I passed the class and got the hell out of there. Mission accomplished, I learned to type and absorbed enough of the rest of the stuff to be able to write a proper business letter. I also learned how to hire a good secretary when the time came, and by then, let a good computer do the rest.

In Canton I had two years of Latin, which was fun and interesting, where I learned a lot of ancient Roman history as well as some of the language. In Asheville I had to choose between French and Spanish, and I chose to take two years of French. The French teacher was a very nice lady who seemed to know the language fairly well, but with one problem as I later learned. When I was in the Army I was sent to Germany and had the opportunity to travel to France and so had the chance to try out my high school French. As anyone who has done this knows, the French love to sneer at Americans who attempt to speak their high school French. The first thing I discovered was that I had actually learned something (surprise). The first time I saw a French newspaper, I picked it up and I could read it; or at least enough of it to get a good sense of what was being said. So that was a start. Eventually I met some people—exactly where and why is a long story for another time and place—with whom I attempted a simple conversation. Between their bad English and my bad French, we were able to communicate enough for them to tell me that my French accent sounded like I was speaking with a distinct American southern drawl. Funny thing, since I had been taught by a woman from North Carolina. She thought she was teaching us this great French accent, but she was putting a southern drawl on it. She—I'd use her name here if I could remember it—would use French art in her lessons, and so I had a terrific introduction to the great French classic art and artists in my two years of French language instruction.

Years later when Sue and I travelled in Europe and France and went to the great museums and I saw these paintings and sculptures and buildings, they were familiar to me, I knew many of their histories because of that French teacher. I always have felt a debt of gratitude to her. She was truly a fine teacher and one of the best I had in high school; even if I couldn't make good grades in her classes, I learned a great deal.

One other note about my French class. We had a soon-to-be famous person who I sat next to and shared homework with. Anyone who reads this and who has been a fan of Miss America may recognize the name Marie Beale Fletcher, Miss America in 1962. She was my classmate and buddy for the year we took French together. She was a nice kid who went on to fame and fortune from Asheville.

That's about all I have to say about high school. It wasn't the Great Experience of my life as it was for some people. I had a couple of close friends. David, whom I've talked about. Sadly, he died of cancer as a relatively young man, and I only saw one time after I graduated high school for a brief visit a few years ago. I never had any girlfriends in high school. There were a few girls, Jewish girls, with whom I was friends, buddies, but none that I would date or go out with. I would occasionally have dates with out-of-town girls when we would attend weekend affairs with BBYO chapters here or in other towns, but nothing serious or interesting came of any of them. Graduation came and went. I skipped the prom.

My driver's license

I turned sixteen on October 17, 1958, and on October 24, I passed my driver's license test. So, of course there has to be a story.

We had moved to Asheville and were operating Asheville Battery Company by now and I had started my junior year at Lee H Edwards High School in Asheville. As I pointed out earlier, I'd been driving since I was at least 14, probably even earlier, so I considered obtaining my license pretty much a formality. In fact, I was fairly resentful of the fact that if we had lived in South Carolina, I'd have had a license for two years already. They were a much more enlightened state, what with fireworks being legal and all.

So, precisely on October 17, my mother took me up to the driver's license office where I went in and announced it was my birthday and I wanted to get my learner's permit, which was the first step. I knew I would need a birth certificate and, unlike my mother, I was prepared, having sent away to the state of Connecticut for it and had it ready. The agent asked if I had taken driver's education or planned to; I said no, as it wasn't a requirement in those days, and that my Dad was teaching me. He asked if I had been studying the manual and was ready for the written test and eye exam? Again, I was ready, and so I passed them and was issued my learner's permit.

For the next week I did ALL the driving. With a learner's permit I was allowed to drive during daylight hours with a licensed adult. No one else was allowed behind the wheel for anything. And in the minimum time allowed by law, seven days, there I was in front of the same agent ready for my road test. In those days you used your own car and could use the car of your choice. I could pretty much drive anything from a farm tractor to a large truck with multiple gears to a car with any kind of transmission, so I didn't think twice about showing up in an old Plymouth station wagon which the store owned with a three-speed stick shift instead of an easier-to-drive sedan with an automatic transmission, the one I planned on becoming my car.

The agent looked up at me (don't forget I was about 6′3″ or so at this time) and said: "Weren't you just here last week?"

Me: "Yes, seven days ago," Maybe a trifle cocky.

Agent: "And you didn't take any driver's ed? You sure you're ready?"

Me: "Yeah, my Dad's a good teacher."

Agent: "Okay, it's your funeral." (or some such encouragement)

Agent (looking at the station wagon): "Where's your car?"

Me: "This green wagon."

Agent: "With the stick shift?"

Me: "Yeah, why? Is that a problem?"

Agent: "For you? Probably. Let's go."

What this guy didn't know, of course, was that I'd been driving this car for months and it had a great transmission and clutch that I was very familiar with. So off we went and he put me through my paces. He tried every maneuver he could think of to make me screw up. Stopping on steep hills, starting on hills, backing up, he even made me parallel park into a space on the side of hill, but Dad really had taught me how to drive and how to do all those maneuvers and I credit him with passing my test.

Dad was so proud of me for getting my driver's license that the next day I had off from school, he loaded up the pickup truck with deliveries of orders the salesmen had sold and sent me out into the country to deliver them. Not only that, but he gave me a sheave of unpaid bills and told me to find as many of these shady characters as I could and collect as much money as I could. Now picture this. Here I am, sixteen years old, going out into the back country of Western North Carolina looking for small town gas stations, garages, and "shade tree" mechanics, delivering merchandise and trying to collect money. No cell phones, no computers, no Google maps. I had written directions, maps, phone numbers, some money in my pocket, and my naïve self-confidence and total belief in myself. Oh yeah, the one thing I keep coming back to—being 6'3" tall, or so—didn't hurt. Well, I delivered everything, and I collected a substantial amount of money as most of the people I found willingly paid at least something on account. I enjoyed myself immensely—my wanderlust has never been sated—and thought my mother would kill my father when she found out what he did. From then on, until I left for college, those delivery runs and debt collections became a regular part of my routine and I never minded doing it.

By the way a shade tree mechanic is some guy who throws a winch—device to hoist an engine out of car—over the branch of big tree over which to haul an engine out from under the hood and does other work under the shade of the tree. He's too poor or fly by night to have a garage to work in.

From cars to college

As Asheville Battery Company slowly faded away in the early '60s, I went away to college in the summer of 1961, to George Washington University in Washington, D.C., after completing my freshman year at Asheville-Biltmore College in Asheville, the precursor to UNC-Asheville. For the next two years, business kept getting progressively worse for Dad, and I'm not sure how they kept me in school.

I worked all the time at various jobs including one I very much enjoyed at a large auto parts wholesaler that had been one of our suppliers. I walked in one day, asked for whoever was responsible for hiring, and announced that I pretty much knew everything about what went on in a store like that and I needed a part time job. He looked at me like I was crazy, but after asking me a number of questions, and since it was inventory time and I quickly showed him that I knew what taking inventory was all about, I was hired on the spot. I worked there, mostly in the warehouse receiving merchandise and stocking shelves, for the two years I was at GWU. I was much happier working than studying.

During the two years I spent at college, there was a parallel story going on at home that would come to affect me later. Dad was apparently talking to Uncle Seymour about returning to Philadelphia and going into business with him. At some point the subject of nursing homes came up. Going into that business sounded promising because Medicare was talked about as a solution to the health care problem for the increasing elderly population; it was a popular topic among the home builders in America who were looking at building nursing homes as new profit centers, if the government was going to start paying for care through these programs called Medicare and Medicaid.

I recall Uncle Seymour coming to Asheville one time to visit, and I went with him and Dad to look at land as possible locations to build a nursing home in Asheville. What a decision THAT would have been! Of course, neither they nor anyone else at the time really knew what they were talking about. Had they done it, they would have been considered geniuses with amazing foresight and made a ton of money. As it is, they missed an opportunity that no one could have realistically foreseen. The years of 1961 and 1962 were too early to see the fortunes to be made 10 years later.

By 1963 it was clear that Asheville Battery Company was on its last legs and wouldn't survive. Mom and Dad decided to once again the sell their house and move on; this time back up north to Philadelphia—a decision that should have been made five years earlier. I don't know the financial implications to them of all this, but I suppose they made out all right on selling the house and the building must have had value, but they lost whatever investment was made in the business. Whether they had done all of this with equity or debt or some combinations, I never asked. It wasn't until years later when I studied and learned real estate and business finance that I even learned what questions that I might have asked. To borrow a famous phrase, "I didn't even know the things I didn't know."

From drive shaft to Army draft

So I'm going to end this tale by telling you that I was drafted by the Army in the summer of 1963, which will be my closing story.

Mom and Dad and Judy and Alan had moved to Philadelphia when I was in my sophomore year at GWU—Mort was away at college—and left the store in the hands of a close friend who tried to keep it going as best he could. He was an old hand at retail business and argued with Dad constantly about the need and benefit of advertising. He was doing some aggressive marketing, but Dad's constant response was that business was so poor that there was no money to pay for it. Dad could never see the cause and effect or the negative feedback loop that he was caught up in.

My third year of college was not very successful, and I was told that I would be allowed back under certain limited circumstances, that I would probably not be able to accumulate sufficient credits to graduate on time, and that I should think about whether I really wanted to come back over the summer. In other words I was on the edge of flunking out, but they'd give me a chance. I hated the whole situation and hid it from everyone, parents included. Dad asked me to go to Asheville and run the store for the summer; I agreed and went to Asheville.

And so the summer came and went, and I was home for a visit sometime in late August and talk of going back to school began. I said I thought I'd take the first semester off because we still needed to figure out how we were going to shut down the store. And, lo and behold, while I was home a letter came in the mail from the Draft Board. Hallelujah! I've been drafted! All my problems solved in one fell swoop! I don't think I put it to them quite that way. You have to understand that this is late in the summer of 1963. Most people had never heard of that strange place in Southeast Asia called Viet Nam, and those who had couldn't pronounce it. We only had a few advisors over there, and it certainly held no danger to a 21-year-old wannabe college dropout who needed an excuse not to go back to school.

And so, I enlisted in the Army for three great years—yes I had a good time in the army—worked for a crazy one-star General who wouldn't let me read Mash or Catch 22, spent two-and-a-half years in Germany, saw a substantial part of the world, visited Israel, lived and worked in Switzerland, and learned enough to get by in three or four languages. I missed going to Viet Nam three different times by sheer dumb luck. Enough stories for now. There are many more to follow. If anybody's interested, let me know and I'll write another book.

Family portrait 1960

Dad, Joe, Morty & Judy somewhere in the mountains of NC circa 1950

Dressed to go out. Probably to a BBYO party Asheville, NC 1959

Afterword

―――――◆―――――

History of Champion's Canton Mill

In 1904, a gentleman by the name of Reuben B. Robertson married Hope Thompson, the daughter of Peter G. Thompson, the organizer of a company called Champion Coated Paper Company of Hamilton, OH. In 1906, as a favor to his financially struggling father-in-law, Reuben Robertson made a trek south, to check out a town called Canton, NC. His trip to Canton was supposed to be a fifty-day exploratory journey during which he could help facilitate the process of building a new pulp mill plant. His fifty-day assignment, however, turned into a lifelong career with Champion. In 1908, Champion Fibre Company opened its door in the town of Canton. Canton was selected based on its proximity to a vast supply of spruce timber, as well as its welcoming political and economic climate. Western North Carolina was an obvious choice for entrepreneurs looking to open up businesses. Above and beyond the advantage of opening a shop in an area with depressed economic conditions, state politicians were paving the way for growth of any kind. In fact, in 1901, the North Carolina General Assembly passed an, "Act to encourage the building of pulp and paper mills and tanneries in the counties of Haywood and Swain." (Bartlett, pp.32) That every corporation, as required by law, every company or firm who may expend one hundred thousand dollars in establishing a factory to convert wood into wood pulp . . . shall not be subject to any criminal prosecution for the pollution of any watercourses upon which such factory or factories are located, and the measure of damages to the owner or owners of lands over which water flows from such factory or factories shall be confined to actual damages, to be ascertained as provided by law.

When the mill opened in 1908, Champion constructed over 60 dwellings to house much of their labor force. This area became known as "Fibreville." Before Champion Fibre Company arrived in 1900, according to the US Census, the town of Canton had 230 residents; by 1910, two years after the opening of the Champion Pulp Mill, Canton was home to 1,393 residents. By 1931, Canton had grown to an industrial town of over 6,000 residents. Champion provided stable employment for the citizens of Canton, and patronage of the local business community kept those not employed by Champion financially afloat as well. It was clear Champion Fibre Company was the lifeblood of Canton, NC. Over the years, Champion Fibre Company went through many name changes. In 1935, it became known as Champion Paper and Fibre Company; later it became Champion Papers, Inc. and then finally Champion International Corporation. After the death of Thompson in 1931, and then his son Logan who died in 1945, Reuben B. Robertson became Champion's Executive Vice President and then its President from 1946 to 1950. Robertson was well liked by all. According to Richard Bartlett, author of Troubled Waters: Champion International and The Pigeon River Controversy, "He was that rare breed of businessmen who could be found in the factory talking shop with his employees, and he was not superficial about it, but talked and listened with knowledge and concern. Old-timers insist that Robertson let it be known that his office door was open to any employee who had something to say, good or bad." (Bartlett, pp.46) Reuben B. Robertson was skilled at keeping his employees happy, which would later prove to be a huge asset to the company. Through the years, the leaders of Champion were extremely happy that Canton had been chosen to be the site of its pulp mill. The rugged lifestyle of the Appalachian culture proved to be a great fit for the

Champion labor force. The region also provided some of the world's best pulpwood. There was one problem though, the river. The Pigeon River was not large enough to absorb and dilute the polluted effluent from the pulp mill. For seven decades, Champion's Canton mill "polluted at will." That is not to say that through the years, lawsuits, studies, and commissions were not brought about because of Champion's relationship with the Pigeon River, but in the 1980s, the concerns of local and regional citizens, environmental groups, and politicians started to be taken a little more seriously. The glory days of North Carolina not discouraging pollution were beginning to slip away. In 1999, after years of environmental litigation, Champion International, was sold to its employees and is now known as the Blue Ridge Paper Company. Today, according to their website, the Canton mill is one of the "ten most environmentally friendly paper plants in the world."

Canton's livelihood

Champion was an asset to the folks of Canton. Located deep within the Smoky and Balsam Mountains, Canton was not easily accessible, and therefore relatively isolated from economic growth. According to some accounts, Champion Paper brought over 10,000 jobs to an area desperate for work. Champion was held in high regard by the citizens of Haywood County because of their labor policies. Champion, unlike other pulp mills, did not want to build a business around high employment turnover. Therefore, employee stability played a huge role in the way Champion developed its business practices. This proved to be beneficial to Champion in more than a few ways. Although it was well known by local citizens that the mill was causing huge environmental problems, the workers supported Champion because they felt valued by the company.

Local Citizen Pinkney Greer Johnson was one voice out of many that had great admiration and support for Champion, even though their business practices were less than favorable towards the natural environment. "Champion and Enka are trying to clean up pollution in the water. Champion spends one million dollars a year (investing in cleaner technology) and has for 20 years. The government must not crucify industry and force it to close with a loss of jobs." (Pinkney Greer Johnson). Pinkney went so far as to claim that the water problems were caused by natural sources. "The water smells, some is brown and looks bad, but this is natural from tree rot."

Over a century ago, a small Tennessee town located downstream from the Champion mill earned the nickname "Widowville," because so many people had died from exposure to toxins. Years later it was determined that the exposure to toxins stemmed from the contaminated fish in the Pi- geon River. Champion would pollute the water, the fish living in the water would pick up the dioxins, humans would catch and eat the fish, hence transferring the dioxins to themselves. Overtime, the dioxins would build up in the humans, causing illnesses such as cancer, and in some cases, death. Above and beyond the public and environmental health effects such as aquatic habitat destruction and palatability of Pigeon River fish, the area has also suffered economic losses as well. There has been an overall decline in property values, tourism, as well as loss of potential income due to businesses choosing to open elsewhere. Raft guide Seth Smith, who grew up in Hartford and still lives there today, recollects about the river. "In the rafting community, it's common to give rivers nicknames. The Nolichucky is the "Chuck," the Nantahala is the "Nanny," but the Pigeon is called the "Dirty Bird." That's the only one where the name gets longer instead of shorter." On rafting trips, which occur twenty-six miles downstream from the mill, Smith talks about how common it is to have brown foam enter the raft. "The kids are a lot quicker to pick up on it than the adults. They ask their parents why there's soap in the water." It's understandable to see why the residents of Cocke County were not happy about the existence of Champion upstream on the river. For the most part, none of them are benefiting from the high paying jobs at the Champion plant, yet they reaping the consequences economically, environmentally, and physically.

Champion knew that in order for it to survive long term, it had to get involved in local politics. After all, it was politics that brought Champion to the region in the first place. It was not until the environmental movement really started to take shape that Champion began to cash in its political chips. With the rise of the environmental awareness in the 1980s, Champion needed protection from the politicians. After all, the economy excuse was no longer holding much weight with most folks. Champion played a role in local, state, and federal politics, and they played it well. At the local level, Champion built itself a "city ring" as described by local citizen, George Coggins.

"The trees and little animals are being killed. Champion is the biggest depositor in the First Union and Wachovia Banks. The banks had to get into politics. D. Hiden Ramsey tried to stop it. "Deacon" Gay Green had the insurance for Champion. They formed a real city "ring" – and Champion is still polluting. They threatened to leave and the city cooperated (or lose 2,000 jobs)." (George Coggins) Champion's most famous political relationship was found with an unlikely politician; Senator Al Gore, a staunch environmental senator from the neighboring state of Tennessee. It was 1987, and Gore was trying his hand at the democratic presidential nomination. He was quoted as saying, before his run for the presidency, that he "looked forward to a day when the Pigeon River will flow clear, pure and clean." He encouraged the EPA to "not budge one inch" on the new tougher water-quality standards that had recently been proposed. But Champion had another thought coming. After all, they knew that if he had any chance of winning the nomination, Gore needed the primary votes from the State of North Carolina. Terry Sanford, the soon to be Governor of North Carolina, was a major supporter of Champion, so Sanford, along with Champion, planned "to change Gore's position." Sources close to Sanford were quoted as saying, "The bottom line for Gore is that he wants to be president and that, when he runs, he'll need a solid Democratic South and he'll need the help . . . of Senator Sanford." North Carolina's political pressure did not end with Sanford. State Representative Jamie Clarke, a major Champion supporter and influential North Carolina Democrat, was holding a fundraiser for his own re-election. Earlier in the month, Gore had written another letter to the EPA attacking Champion, which became public. Gore was scheduled to be a guest speaker at the event, which was going to make it "very difficult" to arrive as one of Clarke's guest. Political maneuvering caused Gore to send Clarke a fax expressing his "regret" over the Champion/EPA problem, and that he would work to produce a "common sense" solution. A few days before the Clarke fundraiser, Gore wrote EPA yet another letter asking for a more permissive water-pollution standard for the Champion mill. Days later, dinner was served at the fundraiser, and Gore was welcomed by the manager of the Champion Plant. Gore's stance change yielded great dividends. He was endorsed by Terry Sanford and Jamie Clarke. Surprisingly enough, Champion helped Gore raise $137,000 in North Carolina alone.

The Pigeon River Controversy

The Pigeon River begins twenty-two miles upstream from Canton, NC, deep within the Pisgah Forest. It starts as a crystal clear water source, attracting fishermen, kayakers, and rafters from all over to enjoy its abundance of clean water, trout, and plant life that inhabit the river. It flows freely, just as nature intended it to do, for over twenty miles, until it reaches Canton. After passing through Canton, the river's color becomes almost coffee black, full of tan foam, and it has a stench similar to that of rotten eggs. Canton's major employer, Champion International, has used the river every day for the past ninety year as a dumping ground for its toxic industrial waste.

Enter Hartford, Tennessee. Hartford has the unfortunate reality of being the first decent-sized community located downstream from the Champion paper mill. Given its location deep within the Smoky Mountains, Hartford should have experienced the same type of economic possibilities as any other mountain town: tourism, vacation homes, whitewater rafting, etc. Instead, it's virtually a ghost town. Folks from the Pigeon Valley communities argue that Champion and the State of North Carolina hold some responsibility for the economic hardships and health issues of the towns located downstream from the mill. They stress that while Canton and the State of North Carolina are the financial recipients of Champions presence in the area, Hartford and the State of Tennessee have come to suffer drastic economic hardships because of it.

In 1985 a historic battle was waged downstream from the plant. The residents of Cocke County Tennessee joined forces with local citizen groups, the media, politicians, and regulatory agencies such as the Environmental Protection Agency (EPA), after North Carolina officials approved a five-year extension of Champion's discharge permit. This permit, issued on May 14, 1985, did not incorporate the water color standards recommended by the EPA. After some back and forth wrangling between Champion and the EPA, Champion's discharge permit was rejected. This left Champion without a valid discharge permit and the State of North Carolina with a company operating "illegally," so on November 8, 1985, the EPA took North Carolina's permit issuing authority away and demanded that the paper mill clean up its act. It looked as if, for the first time in

Champion's seven decade history in North Carolina, Champion was going to be unable to finagle its way out of environmental accountability.

As cheers of joy were heard across state lines, panic struck in the town of Canton. Champion, who was the town's lifeblood, made it very clear that it was in no financial position to invest the type of money into new environmentally friendly technology, and if push came to shove, they would have to shut their doors. This meant, as the town's largest employer, that many residents faced the unfortunate prospect of losing their jobs as well as their homes. The panic did not just stop with Champion employees. Local businesses, which depended on Champion's employees, also became unnerved at the prospect of losing the mill.

EPA public hearings became like circus rings as mobs of differing sides flooded the meeting halls. In 1988, the controversy reached a high point when Tennessee's then-Senator Al Gore, who was seeking the democratic nomination, intervened on behalf of Champion. Gore asked the EPA, to work with Champion to come to a common sense solution to the ongoing pollution problem. To most Tennesseans, Gore, who was known as being a pro-environment senator, had sold out his home state in the quest for the primary votes in North Carolina.

Looking as if Champion had yet another reprieve from stricter water quality regulations, pressure from environmental groups amplified. Champion, realizing that the controversy over the Pigeon River was not going away, began taking drastic measures to reduce toxic emissions into the river. According to some accounts, by 1994, Champion had invested over $330 million dollars in new, environmentally friendly technology. By 1999, the financial burden of the environmental regulations had taken its toll on Champion. The company sold the plant to its employers, and it is now called Blue Ridge Paper Company.

With all the money spent and energy put towards the cleaning up of the Pigeon River, conditions have improved. That said, to this day, neither party is able to let the issue relax. From Champion's (now Blue Ridge Paper) standpoint, they can proudly claim that a 99% reduction in dioxin level has occurred in the river, since the clean up process began over twenty years ago. In fact, they can also state that in early 2007 advisory boards deemed fish caught in the Pigeon River safe for consumption.

However, environmental groups, such as the Dead Pigeon River Council, challenge the Pigeon River success story. The environmental groups are quick to point out that nowhere else in the world, is there a mill the size of Champion on a river as small as the Pigeon. Up until recently, one of the main EPA water monitoring stations on the Pigeon River was located just after Lake Waterville. This allowed a huge amount of dilution of the toxic pollution to occur before the water actually reached the monitoring station. Most poignantly stated that while, yes, the water is clearer, it is still not a natural color.

So, while the Pigeon River Controversy may be in a state of lull right now, rest assured that as long as there is a paper mill located on the river, the issue will never fade. Every five years, when the discharge permit is set to reissue, the folks of Cocke County, get together to keep the issue alive. Conversely, the employees of Blue Ridge Paper company keep working hard to ensure that their livelihood remains in their hometown of Canton, North Carolina.

Paper mill in 2015

Bibliography

Chapter 1: How did we get to Canton anyway?

Polonsky, Antony. "History of the Jews of Eastern Europe." The Jews in Poland and Russia. Volume II: 1881 to 1914.

Kirsch, Adam. The New Republic, Sept 2010. http://www.newrepublic.com/book/review/tumultuous-timepoland-russia-jews-polonsky

Kucinskas, David. "Texas History 101 in 1907, Nine Hundred Immigrants Passed Through Galveston." Texas Magazine. http://www.texasmonthly.com/story/texashistory-101-1

www.ingramcontent.com/pod-product-compliance
Lightning Source LLC
Chambersburg PA
CBHW072013110526
44592CB00012B/1291